D0542762

INTERNATIONAL COMMUNITY

A Goal for A
New World Order

George C. McGhee

Series Editor
Kenneth W. Thompson

Volume 1
In the Miller Center Series on
A New World Order

UNIVERSITY
PRESS OF
AMERICA

Lanham • New York • London

The Miller Center

University of Virginia

Copyright © 1992 by
University Press of America®, Inc.
4720 Boston Way
Lanham, Maryland 20706

3 Henrietta Street
London WC2E 8LU England

Co-published by arrangement with
The Miller Center of Public Affairs,
University of Virginia

The views expressed by the author(s) of this publication do not necessarily
represent the opinions of the Miller Center. We hold to Jefferson's dictum that:
"Truth is the proper and sufficient antagonist to error, and has nothing to
fear from the conflict, unless by human interposition, disarmed of her
natural weapons, free argument and debate."

Library of Congress Cataloging-in-Publication Data

McGhee, George Crews, 1912–
International community : a goal for a new world order /
George C. McGhee.
p.   cm. — (Miller Center series on a new world order : v. 1)
1. International organization.   I. Title.   II. Series.
JX1954.M39   1991   341.2—dc20   92–10570 CIP

ISBN 0–8191–8538–8 (cloth : alk. paper)
ISBN 0–8191–8539–6 (pbk. : alk. paper)

The paper used in this publication meets the minimum requirements of
American National Standard for Information Sciences—Permanence
of Paper for Printed Library Materials, ANSI Z39.48–1984.

Dedicated

to my

Grandchildren

Table of Contents

APPENDIXES (Cont.)

Preface

Kenneth W. Thompson

Americans are often criticized for moving toward isolationism and for a retreat from international responsibility. The polls suggest that support for President George Bush has declined because his critics say he has emphasized foreign policy at the expense of domestic policy. Problems of the cities are ignored while the economic development of Third World and former Communist countries is assigned high priority. The editor of the leading international relations journal, *Foreign Affairs*, urges less attention to foreign issues and more to urgent domestic problems.

One way of contributing to the national discussions in this area is to consider the views of former officials and scholars who defend a continued sense of international responsibility by Americans. Since the Gulf War, much of the discussion has found a focus in proposals for a New World Order. Indeed, President Bush has invoked this concept in explaining the basis for the action against Saddam Hussein. Some who called on the United Nations to respond to Saddam's aggression against Kuwait did so in the language of World Order.

Because the idea has figured more prominently in 1991 than at any time since the immediate post-World War

II period, institutes concerned with world peace and international cooperation bear an obligation to encourage public discussion on the subject. Inasmuch as the Miller Center is such a center, we have explored possible contributions we could make.

At least three approaches are possible, and we contemplate Forums and some publications in each of these areas. The first approach is to be responsive to a proposal for a clearly defined formulation on the need for some kind of world order. The second would be an intensive scholarly analysis of the many dimensions and historical experiences with such approaches. Finally, it would be helpful to consider discussions which examine in depth obstacles and problems that arise in contemplating a New World Order.

Three such studies are underway and the first is exemplified in the present study by Ambassador George McGhee of *International Community*. McGhee's proposal is subtitled *A Goal for a New World Order*. It is noteworthy that proposals of this kind often follow war and international conflict. Equally significant, the authors of such proposals are often senior leaders and officials who have held major positions in time of war and peace. Two earlier leaders who come to mind are President Woodrow Wilson during and after World War I and General Douglas MacArthur after World War II.

The importance of defining the goals of a New World System is that hard-pressed incumbents who advance them are unlikely to be specific. Both the press of official duties and national and international political pressures make such efforts problematical. Once leaders leave office they are freer to undertake more detailed inquiries. This is obviously the case with Ambassador McGhee.

PREFACE

It should be clear that calls to action are likely to be controversial. Their substance is the articulation and defense of a viewpoint, not the careful weighing of alternatives. In the language of the academy, such efforts are not research papers. That kind of effort will follow in a volume organized around the scholarly conclusions of Professor I. L. Claude of the University of Virginia. Both approaches are valid and will encourage serious thought. Our series begins with Ambassador McGhee but will continue through published statements of competing ideas and approaches.

During and following the war in the Persian Gulf, President Bush referred on many occasions to our goal as the New World Order. Ambassador George McGhee has come today to tell us what a New World Order might be.

His story has been one of success both in the private and in the public sector. Following a Rhodes scholarship and a Ph.D. from Oxford University, he began his career as a registered professional engineer, a subsurface geologist for Atlantic Refining Company, and an independent explorer and oil producer. He was a partner in De Golyer, MacNaughton, and McGhee, and later the owner of McGhee Production Company. In these capacities he established a reputation throughout the private sector.

However, he also has served in the public sector as an official of the War Production Board and of the Combined Raw Materials Board. From 1947 to 1949, he was coordinator for aid to Greece and Turkey. He has held three ambassadorships—to the Federal Republic of Germany, to Turkey, and as ambassador-at-large. He was an assistant secretary and then undersecretary of state for political affairs.

PREFACE

Ambassador McGhee is the author of *Envoy to the Middle World*. He also is the catalyst who encouraged some of us to participate in a project that led to the publication of *National Interest and Global Goals*.

It is a tribute to him and perhaps a measure of interest in the subject that he has inspired and launched this series on a New World Order.

Overview

With the failure of the U.S.S.R. and the end of the Cold War, a new period of history is in the making. The drastic changes that have been occurring have stimulated discussions on how to create a more peaceful and stable world. The term *New World Order* has emerged, chosen by President George Bush after the U.S.-led U.N. victory in the Gulf War. Although this term is appealing, it has not been clearly defined, and so there is ambiguity about whether it represents a desirable end result or a strategy for achieving one. It has, however, inspired a useful search for what might be better termed a new world system.

At present the world faces many severe international problems. A coherent framework for approaching these problems, however, is lacking; the efforts that are being made do not appear to be guided by any unifying concept of a new world system. The end of the Cold War has eliminated the threat of Soviet aggression; however, it has ushered in new problems, economic competition, civil wars, and mass migrations, along with problems inherited from the past. Suitable plans and resources have not yet been available to transform the new states of Eastern Europe and the remnants of the Soviet Union into democracies with market economies. Despite European Community assistance, little progress is being made in eliminating conflicts resulting from the threatened dissolution of

Yugoslavia. Valiant U.S. efforts have resulted in continuing Middle East negotiations, but no breakthrough has occurred in resolving the Arab-Israeli dispute and other problems in the region.

We have the opportunity today to create a new world system based on past experience, current realities, and future possibilities. We will analyze the drastic changes that have taken place in world power centers, in the roles of balance of power and balance of restraint, in the perils of the international arms trade, and the new role the United States can be expected to play in a new world system. Short- and medium-term steps to create a new world system are proposed, and comments on such a system are put forth by experts. We must identify types of international problems for which solutions could be undertaken, find the means to apply ready and effective sanctions against those who threaten world peace, and agree on procedures for the application of force in the event that all other measures fail. Throughout emphasis is placed on a multilateral approach, with reliance on cooperation between major democracies.

And finally, I advance the rationale that a lasting new world system can only come through the strengthening of international community–bonds of community developed and organized on a global scale as it has been on a more limited basis in, for example, the European Community. Steps that would help create a true international community based on nations practicing democracy and respect for human rights, are described. The highly important relationship between national and international goals is also addressed, and further elaborated on in the reprinted text in Appendix II.

Crafting a New World System: The Initial Steps

It is widely believed that the nations of the world must now, with the end of the Cold War, seek to establish a new modern world system to manage the relationships that are replacing past East-West and North-South confrontations. There has emerged a new world of interdependent nations, increasingly democratic and dedicated to a market economy, with high technology and instant communications. The United States and the successors to the U.S.S.R. have abandoned their bitter rivalry and undertaken normal diplomatic relations. A true European Community has been created, and Eastern Europe has been freed from communism. On the other hand, although the nations of the world are being relieved of the crushing burdens of the Cold War race, they face grave economic and environmental problems. What future awaits a world that has outgrown its old stage and is ready to pursue new goals?

We have come to a watershed in history, to a point that is dominated more by the future than the past. For the United States, having without seeking it emerged from the U.S.-Soviet confrontation as the single greatest world power, the responsibility for leadership is particularly awesome. The United States, President George Bush has said, seeks "new ways of working with other nations to deter aggression, and to achieve stability, prosperity, and above all, peace."

Since the Gulf War provides the best example of President Bush's idea of a New World Order in action, it deserves special study for the lessons it offers. The U.S.-led U.N. coalition created to oust the Iraqi forces that had on 1 August 1990 invaded Kuwait, included most U.N. members, 16 of which contributed armed forces. The world reaction to the Iraqi seizure proved that the United Nations had, under U.S. leadership and with other major power support, the ability to act quickly and effectively in stopping the aggression. For the first time the United Nations applied the powerful sanctions of boycott and embargo against an aggressor, and during the Gulf War the U.N. blockade and embargo produced at least a demonstrable effect. Although there is now no foreseeable threat of another major war, we should all recognize that, if any new aggression is not stopped by threats of retaliation, we must be prepared to provide whatever level of military force is required.

The nations that led the U.N. coalition were described in terms of a new role—"Guarantors of International Order"—by the leaders of the seven largest democracies meeting in London in July 1991. Citing the Gulf War as an example of this role in practice, they affirmed that the international community had demonstrated its ability to act together "to restore international peace and security and to resolve conflict." They held that the community must build on this success, striving for cooperation "not just in the Middle East but wherever danger and conflict threaten or other challenges must be met." They highlighted the U.N. role in imposing sanctions against Iraq and called for revitalization of the United Nations, with preventive diplomacy and peacekeeping as top priorities. Accordingly, they also called on the United Nations to establish a registry for international arms transactions.

The July 1991 economic summit also expressed agreement on actions to be taken on a number of persistent political problems around the world. They included: support for a Middle East Peace Conference to settle the Arab economic boycott against Israel and the Israeli building of settlements on occupied Arab lands; agreement that sanctions should continue against Iraq until it complies with U.N. resolutions settling the Gulf War and establishing the right of Iraqis to choose their leadership; agreement that Iraq should not become a nuclear power; and preparation for a meeting of the seven with Soviet President Mikhail Gorbachev. The dismantling of apartheid in South Africa was welcomed and support expressed for a decision by the Yugoslav people about their future form of government.

Perhaps these agreements may be considered a by-product if not a part of some kind of new world system in the making. They at least provide fresh proof that a consensus can be achieved among leading democracies, and that they can share leadership and responsibility. This was also confirmed by European and U.S. efforts to alleviate the plight of the Kurdish and Shiite refugees created by the Gulf War. In addition, as an independent action that might be cited, the nations of the world, separately and through the United Nations, responded quickly and generously to the tragic aftermath of tornadoes and flooding in

Bangladesh, which resulted in at least 200,000 deaths. This action in particular demonstrates a spirit going beyond cooperation to deter aggression, suggesting a new world in which nations could call upon each other for help in other vital matters, with the expectation of a positive response.

The need for a new world system, with the United States playing an important role, was recognized by the conclusion of the Seventy-Ninth American Assembly in May 1991:

> A concert of powers working together, and a world of independent nations equal before the law . . . between them provide the most fruitful guide to an American policy. The United States will need to act in concert with other major powers in order to sustain a stable balance, indeed its citizens will demand that it do so, but it will also need to work with the U.N. and other intergovernmental organizations, showing respect for other sovereign states and their legal rights. Only in extreme cases of emergency or humanitarian need will it be right to set aside the sovereignty of other states. . . . A community of peaceable democracies . . . reflects an aspiration and an ideal. America must promote the adoption of liberal democratic values.

The essence of major power cooperation is a sharing of decision-making and the burdens created. The powers participating in the Gulf War coalition provide an example. With the United States as acknowledged leader and support in part from the U.S.S.R., other non-Gulf military contributions were made by the United Kingdom, France, and Italy. Germany and Japan gave the most substantial support as outside powers, but no military support for legal reasons and less political support for not being members of the U.N. Security Council. It is generally agreed that both restraints should be corrected. The Arab states principally involved, particularly Saudi Arabia, provided both military and financial support. Chinese support was indifferent.

Future coalitions will be expected to be tailored to the problems and states included. The North European democracies and the major Commonwealth countries, Australia and Canada, could all lend political, if not financial and military support. The major Far Eastern states, apart from Japan, remain in doubt.

We must first consider how to go about crafting a new world system, which implies a bold new approach to resolving world problems through multilateral action, but which has not been clearly defined in terms of scope or ultimate goals. The obvious general goals of such a system might include: world peace and security against aggression; the expansion of democracy, human rights, and political and economic freedom under a rule of law and order; improvement in the education, health, and well-being of peoples; progress in resolving environmental problems that concern us all; and the protection of every nation's rights to internal diversity, including national pride and a separate way of life. Far from suggesting that the world try to improve itself in all of these respects at once, I believe that progress requires intensive study over time, creative solutions, and the commitment of substantial resources.

As a new world system is being created, we must seek to deter threatened aggression by all possible means. Techniques must be developed by consensus for coercive actions that can be employed rapidly and effectively. Economic sanctions may offer the best vehicle for an initial response—for example: the freezing of foreign assets, denial of investment and credit, and embargo and blockade against trade. Such sanctions might be followed by denial of rights to air and sea access; and use of tele-communications, pipelines, and power lines. To be sure, this subject has received much consideration in the past with limited success. Today, however, it offers a greater challenge as nations seek to reshape their global relationships.

As noted earlier, economic sanctions may be used to good effect, but they may also prove limited in a given situation. On 5 December 1990, William Webster, director of the Central Intelligence Agency, told Congress that Iraq's military could maintain its current combat readiness for no more than nine months if economic sanctions continued to hold, and that the ability of the Iraqi air force to fly regular missions could decline within three months. Webster predicted that mounting shortages caused by the sanctions were likely to shut down all but Iraq's energy-related and military industries by the spring and "almost certainly" by the summer of 1991. Yet the sanctions did not appear adequate to force an Iraqi withdrawal from Kuwait, or to stop Saddam Hussein's efforts to produce atomic weapons.

Consequently, the military option cannot be ruled out, and we must consider now how to maximize its effectiveness, and determine what may be required. For example, in some cases a military operation may be best conducted on a regional basis by ad hoc delegation of U.N. authority to specific countries, or to regional security organizations created under the U.N. Charter, such as the North Atlantic Treaty Organization (NATO). The United Nations must, however, continue to be the body any nation can turn to in the event of a threat of aggression, a natural catastrophe, or other serious problem, with the final determination of the appropriate response to be made by the U.N. Security Council or other U.N. body.

Consideration must also be given to how coalitions or other responses to international emergencies should be organized and conducted, bearing in mind the valuable lessons of the Gulf War. Any actions authorized by the Security Council should be preceded by consultation among participants. Prior agreement should be arrived at, wherever possible, about how the operation will be financed, its goals, and the latitude that will be allowed those responsible for the conduct of the operation. In repelling major acts of aggression, U.S. leadership may be necessary for success; however, the United States must give careful thought to how its authority is exercised and the rights given to other major contributors. Even minor nations involved will feel they have the right to some input.

Finally, we must address the difficult question of when U.N. or other multilateral intervention would be justified within the borders of a member country. The United Nations has in the past been reluctant to intervene in such cases, and Common Market, United States, and United Nations intervention in Yugoslavia as of this writing has not been effective. At least a codification should be developed of the types of situations that would justify such intervention on behalf of the international community. These might include, for example, large-scale genocide, as in the Sudan, or hopeless internal armed power struggles, as in Liberia. The African states set an example by sending troops to stop the bloodshed in Liberia. A U.N. peacekeeping force has arrived in Cambodia to protect the people against warring political groups. The appropriateness of multilateral intervention, however, will increasingly become an issue in connection with a host of international nonaggression problems. We need to begin asking, for example, to what extent should illegal mass movements of peoples from overpopulated areas such as Haiti, and in such circumstances as those experienced by the "boat people" of Vietnam, justify international intervention. This may in the future be the main threat of invasion. Should multilateral intervention be employed to prevent destruction of the Brazilian rain forests, the effects of the loss of the ozone layer, damage by acid rain, or severe threats of famine, pestilence, and disease? Criteria for reaction to non-war multilateral interventions would constitute a vital component in the framework of a new world system.

In Chapter 4 I will present the views of many who have considered the question of a new world system in depth.

Revising World Threat Perceptions

The end of the 20th century appears to promise a climate of peace, an unusual prospect both welcome and yet difficult for many to believe. For almost 60 continuous years—from 1930, when Japan first threatened Manchuria, to 1990, when the U.S.S.R. gave up Eastern Europe—the overriding fact of life for most of the world was war or the threat of war, posed at different times by three totalitarian states with massive military strength and an appetite for conquest. This cumulative threat by Japan, Germany, and the U.S.S.R., made a deep impression on three generations, so deep that it is now hard for us to grasp that it no longer exists.

These years of confrontation were experienced in a dramatic way by the United States, notwithstanding its geographical distance from the primary centers of conflict. Originally settled by people whose aim was to assure their right to live out their lives in peace and freedom, America nevertheless became involved in two major wars. After being drawn by European ties into World War I and winning, Americans were compelled to undertake again in

World War II a massive defense effort to counter the combined threat of the Japanese and German quests for empire. With its European allies, the United States made the long, painful effort to achieve military superiority over the Axis powers, only to find that the Soviet Union, presumably an ally, was using the forces it had created to defeat Germany to build its own world communist empire.

I myself was involved for three years in the war, ending in Guam with the U.S. B-29 air war against Japan; for the next 22 years I participated in the new war, the Cold War, in the U.S. diplomatic service's effort to contain communism in Greece, Turkey, the Middle East, South Asia, Africa, and Germany. These decades of global great power war and the threat of nuclear war, massive military forces and budgets, heavy casualties, and no holds barred covert intelligence operations, had a deep effect on me. They still tend, I believe, to dominate American thinking. We must learn to throw out this Cold War psychology. We must not be "bad winners."

So long accustomed to Cold War realities, many Americans seem to have difficulty in accepting new policies more suitable to the problems we face in a period which appears to offer an indefinite peace. By Cold War policies I mean more than just defense policy. American efforts to contain communism had an overwhelming impact on the whole spectrum of U.S. policies toward other nations. This goes beyond assistance to U.S. allies to repair damages from World War II and to avoid future wars, to participation in the Korean and Vietnam wars, to U.S. military and economic assistance to most of the world's countries through such programs as Greek-Turkish aid, the Marshall Plan, NATO, and Mutual Defense Assistance. Our military alliances, NATO, the Southeast Asia Treaty

Organization, the Central Treaty Organization, and the Organization of American States all bear testimony to the scope of the U.S. role in the Cold War. Even economic and development assistance to the Third World, sometimes viewed as an expression of U.S. generosity, has in fact been largely intended to keep these nations from going communist.

The Cold War is over, and we must now draw up a blueprint for a new world system based on new security concepts. With the elimination of old massive threats, we overcame the need to maintain the forces that were created to meet them. Further, the prospect of peace has been favored by the great reduction of Iraqi military power during the Gulf War, a unique case not likely to be repeated. A need, however, will continue for defense forces to take care of minor trouble spots and unexpected contingencies not related to the Cold War. Gadhafi of Libya and Noriega of Panama have demonstrated, unfortunately, that there can always be mad dictators whom we must be prepared to deal with.

These remaining threats, however, can in no way be comparable to the direct security threat once posed by Japan, Germany, and the U.S.S.R. Japan and Germany are now democracies and allies. The Soviet military threat collapsed with the Soviet internal economic and political failure; a democratic election has made Boris Yeltsin president of the U.S.S.R.'s greatest state; the Soviet Communist party has been disbanded; and democratic political parties with broad appeal are being formed. The threat of a rightist coup overthrowing the Soviet government has been virtually eliminated by the 72-hour, unsuccessful seizure of power by the Communist party, the army, and the KGB on 18 August 1991. If this group could

11

not succeed against the popular opposition led by President Yeltsin, it should not be possible for any other coalition to do so in an increasingly democratic Russia.

With Iraq and Iran largely defanged by war and China preoccupied with population and many other pressing problems, there are no nondemocratic nations left in the world that have the military power, much less the incentive, to threaten U.S. or world security. The Gulf War showed that the democratic powers and supporting nations are willing and able to stop an aggression much more powerful than anything they might face in the future. With Soviet support no longer available to proxy states, future coalitions would not be burdensome to any one nation, including the United States. There is no nation in the Western Hemisphere, which is composed mostly of democracies and allies, that could constitute a threat to the United States or to each other. Only Cuba ever presented any real threat, and this "worst-case" has done the United States little harm.

If this estimate continues to be confirmed, I believe the United States can safely implement substantial reductions in the military budgets and forces of the Cold War years, beyond those already scheduled in "Star Wars," U.S. forces in Europe, and major U.S. ships. In the absence of a potential enemy with high-tech weapons, the United States does not require sophisticated weapons such as the Stealth bomber, which was built to defend against the Soviet Union. It will, however, continue to be morally incumbent on the United States to contribute its share to any united effort at the new reduced levels, to avoid war, or wage it successfully if war is unavoidable.

I believe there remains no reason why the United States cannot in the foreseeable future shift massive resources from the military budget to the needs of education, health, housing, environment, and national infrastructure. It is time for policymakers to ask, in response to every defense budget request, "Whom are we preparing to fight?" For example, "Why do we need bases in the Philippines when we have no potential Pacific Ocean naval enemy and have bases in Guam and Hawaii?"

It is also time, I believe, for us to consider a revision of our traditional concept of Balance of Power and to think more in terms of Balance of Restraint. The buildup of any strong potential enemy would take a long time, under continuous world scrutiny. Improved intelligence should detect it, and steps could be taken by the world democracies, preferable through the United Nations, to stop it.

Balance of Power is a military concept that reached prominence in Europe during the Metternich era of the 19th century. Insofar as it represented a balance between comparable opposing military forces deployed around central Europe, having ready access to each other and known human and economic resources behind them, a true Balance of Power could indeed be analyzed and often achieved. I question whether Balance of Power, in a unipolar world in which the United States is, by a wide margin, the leading military power, is as relevant as what might be termed a Balance of Restraint.

There can in a strict sense be no balance between forces that differ in kind or are not in direct confrontation. One can compare numbers of combatants and firepower of weapons but not, in any simple equation, such factors as the problems of transportation, morale of troops, opportunities for sabotage, or national resolve. Worldwide, the Balance of Power analogy breaks down. Furthermore, international defense problems will consist increasingly of local disputes between small powers and derived from bitter, inherited differences such as those in Palestine, Cambodia, Sri Lanka, and Northern Ireland. With the end of the Cold War the small powers have increasing freedom to ignore advice or attempts to coerce them to make peace.

An appropriate reorientation of policy to prevent future conflict will thus result in less emphasis on Balance of Power and more on a Balance of Restraint, on the basis of a credible plan to keep the peace. Unlike Balance of Power, usually achieved by a balancing *up* by a mutual increase in military levels, Balance of Restraint balances *down*, by a mutual diminution of power leading to a relaxation of tension and to peace. In the past this was done through nuclear test bans and nonproliferation agreements and bilateral U.S.-Soviet treaties limiting nuclear and conventional forces. Efforts to increase restraints are less likely to result in tests of strength and more likely to promote the trust upon which to build cooperative relationships.

Organizations founded with such a restraining purpose in mind already exist, for nonmilitary reasons as well as military reasons. The United States, in particular, could be compared to the sleeping giant of *Gulliver's Travels*, who was bound in his sleep by the Lilliputians. America's freedom to use its military and economic strength has been bound by cords that it helped create—by institutions such as the United Nations, the International Monetary Fund, and the World Court.

A world whose stability depends more on a Balance of Restraint will eventually become a much safer world. The more broadly based and the lower its military levels, the more generally acceptable it will become. The threat of any state will necessarily diminish as multilateral mechanisms and world opinion play a greater role. Multilateral efforts, such as those that recently helped remove Cuban and Soviet forces from Angola, will be facilitated.

World leaders will have to focus on alleviating long-term conflicts where grave injustice is perceived by one or both of the parties involved, as in Northern Ireland, Palestine, and Sri Lanka. A determined effort must be made to change the political framework that has prevented a solution. Committees of Inquiry composed of impartial world leaders might, after objective study, propose new, perhaps drastic solutions, which alone can help resolve ancient, deeply held animosities. Such drastic steps may be needed as General de Gaulle's bold withdrawal from Algeria, or the exchange of 3.5 million Greeks and Turks from each other's lands by the Treaty of Lausanne. For the same reasons the economic disparity between the developed and developing world, and restrictions on human rights, must also be lowered to reduce tensions. These persisting issues, which have undermined any basis for progress in many places, are the prime candidates for receiving resources and energies freed by the end of the Cold War.

Control over the international sale of arms represents another major area of concern that must be addressed by a new world system. Eighty-five percent of the large military items in 1990 were produced by only five countries: the United States, the Soviet Union, the United Kingdom, France, and China. Control of this trade poses serious difficulties in peace as well as in war. Demand for conventional arms is not limited to international rivalries, including the border disputes that take place between many of the contiguous nations of the world. Every state requires sufficient military strength to maintain domestic law and

15

order, a fact of life that has often been demonstrated both by democratic governments in fear of military coups and by military dictators seeking to discourage military rivals or dissident democratic groups. Limiting the purchase of arms to the needs of legitimate self-defense depends upon the cooperation of the major sellers.

The already difficult task of limiting arms sales is becoming more complicated by the empowerment of countries—even those in the preindustrial stage of development—to manufacture their own arms. Further, whereas a key incentive for much of past arms sales was the containment of communism, which is no longer a problem, today's sales are for profit. Greater competition in arms sales in Asia is occurring with Japanese and Indian participation. Since 1990 sales of the five principal countries mentioned were down a third from 1989 sales, the seller countries are under pressure from arms producers to sell more and more. Thus, many sellers feel obligated not only to meet the arms demands of key allies and long-time customers, but to prevent job losses and increasing taxes and foreign exchange from arms sales. In addition, most countries feel compelled to maintain a healthy arms industry to handle future possible demands, regardless of any present decrease in domestic military requirements. For these reasons, most seller countries are resisting worldwide limits to arms sales.

At the 1991 economic summit world leaders did not move to embargo arms shipments to the Middle East which the United States had earlier proposed, even though a precedent for doing so had been set following the Arab-Israeli war of 1947. To justify the relaxation of their wartime arms embargo and to prevent an arms race, the United States, United Kingdom, and France signed the

Tripartite Declaration of 1950, which placed strict control over these countries' shipments to the Middle East in the hands of a special committee in London. However, as already mentioned, the 1991 summit did call on the United Nations to establish a registry for international arms transactions that would give notice of any attempts "to build up holdings of conventional weapons beyond a reasonable level." This was a responsible step in the right direction. Such a registry would be a useful supplement to the existing bilateral treaties (largely between the United States and the Soviet Union) and to the control over nuclear weapons available, at least in theory, to signatories of the Nuclear Nonproliferation Treaty through the International Atomic Energy Agency in Vienna.

The industrialized nations, particularly the five mentioned above, must now also make a serious effort at protecting themselves from control by their own arms industries. This danger was something that President Dwight D. Eisenhower understood very well and specifically warned against in his farewell address. He knew that weapons requirements could be claimed not only in the national interest but by heavily subsidized industry lobbies that were effective in influencing the platforms of political parties. Recent scandals of widespread bribery in connection with contracts for military production further highlight the need for reform. World leaders must take a new look at whether we need all the weapons that are being forced on us. Arms can be the cause as well as the result of wars.

CHAPTER THREE

The New U.S. Role

The question of U.S. leadership in the world has been complex and susceptible to rapid and radical change. Until Western Europe was threatened by Hitler, Americans had little desire to exercise leadership outside the Western Hemisphere. After World War II, the United States continued in a leadership role because it was the only country to survive the war with a healthy economy, the economies of most of the other world powers having suffered severe losses. Faced with the new threat of communism, the United States was forced to defend the free world it had helped save, providing the necessary leadership and resources until the political and economic bankruptcy of the Soviet Union in 1990 removed that threat.

Then came the world crisis posed by Saddam Hussein's aggression against Kuwait, and the United States elected to exercise a leadership role again, despite economic hardship at home and the fact that it did not seek world leadership. It was clear that if the United States did not take the lead, no other nation could have or would have done so. The U.S. role was accepted, with those most

19

able (Germany, Japan, and the Gulf oil states) paying most of the cost.

A similar U.S. role in future comparable situations cannot be assured, however, since it would not necessarily be endorsed by other nations or by the American people. Consideration of an appropriate U.S. role in the New World Order must take stock both of the lessons of the Gulf War episode and of the mood of the American public. Key members of the coalition believed that U.S. leadership was at times forced or exercised without adequate consultation. And now that the United States has restored its national confidence by demonstrating to the world its ability to lead and win a difficult war, it is uncertain whether most Americans would be willing to make such an effort again, particularly if the United States had to pay its full share.

It is important to remember also that the formidable threat posed by Saddam Hussein was a unique case—aggression by a small, semideveloped country of only 18 million people, which had managed to become the sixth largest military power in the world under the control of a ruthless military dictator. Saddam Hussein's aggression also jeopardized control of at least 20 percent of world oil, and as much as 40 percent if Saudi Arabia was to be taken. Further, the conflict involved states that were willing and able to pay most of the bill in order to survive. Given all these facts, Americans largely supported U.S. leadership in resolving the situation.

Leading analysts, however, hold that there is widespread evidence that the American people do not want to be "policemen of the world," that they want to stay at home and use the limited resources available to the U.S. government to face up to the country's many domestic problems. The words of the Democratic leader in the Senate, George Mitchell (D-Maine), spoken in response to President Bush's 1991 State of the Union address, depicted an America that is tired, in debt, and more eager to lay down its external burdens than at any other time in the last 50 years.

Various national commentators have made similar observations about the current trend in American thinking. For example, Strobe Talbott wrote in the 29 July issue of *Time*:

> The American labor movement is in a protectionist mood. So are many members of Congress. Local officials, bedeviled by deficits and cutbacks, fulminate at the idea of U.S. aid to the former evil empire. At a recent meeting of the National League of Cities, Sidney Barthelemy, the mayor of New Orleans, said, "The Federal Government needs to shift its priorities from continuing to assist and aid everybody outside America [while] ignoring the problems inside America."

In May, William Hyland, editor of *Foreign Affairs*, wrote a guest column for the *New York Times* in which he called on the United States to "start selectively disengaging" from overseas commitments and in which he called for "a psychological turn inward" and a Marshall Plan "to put our house in order." Four weeks later, the *Times'* own James Reston argued that "the main threat to our nation's security [comes] from within," and he urged President Bush to build a "new American order." Meanwhile, Peter Peterson, chairman of the Council on Foreign Relations and the Institute of International Economics, advocated "the primacy of the domestic agenda."

In the July issue of *Atlantic*, Alan Tonelson of the Economic Strategy Institute, a Washington think tank, denounced the "irrelevance of our recent foreign policy, and even its victories, to the concerns of most Americans." He went on to say that the United States should junk the idea of "exercising something called leadership" and "insulate" itself from the disasters of the Third World. He would also have the United States abandon "overseas missions that, however appealing, bear only marginally on protecting and enriching the nation." Activities that he believes qualify for U.S. attention include "promoting peace, stability, democracy and development around the world" and "protecting human rights."

Jeane Kirkpatrick, President Reagan's ambassador to the United Nations, recently wrote that "it is time to give up the dubious benefits of superpower status, time to give up the unusual burdens of the past and return to normal times." That means, she said, taking "care of pressing problems of education, family, industry and technology" at home. That means further, she indicated, that the United States should not try to be the balancer of power in Europe or in Asia or try to shape the political evolution of the Soviet Union. Instead, America should aspire to be "a normal country in a normal time."

Similarly, other commentators have suggested that in the absence of a serious threat to the nation or the world, the United States should relax, that it should not try to lead everybody or run everything in the world, that it should cooperate with other nations on a more equal basis, and that it should devote more of its efforts to solving domestic problems, many of which depend on international cooperation for success. As a minority of at least one, Charles Krauthammer disagrees, and it is interesting to note the argument he advanced in an article entitled "The Unipolar Moment," which was published in the 1990-91 issue of *Foreign Affairs: America and the World*.

> International stability is never a given. It is never the norm. When achieved it is the product of self-conscious action by the great powers, and most particularly of the greatest power, which now and for the foreseeable future is the United States. . . . We are in for abnormal times. Our best hopes for safety in such times as in difficult times past, is in American strength and will to lead a unipolar world, unashamedly laying down the rules of world order and prepared to enforce them.

Krauthammer's words are heady stuff—Teddy Roosevelt at his best. And there has been some evidence that the Bush administration was thinking in such terms when it attempted to suggest solutions to the civil wars in Ethiopia and Yugoslavia. Nevertheless, apart from being unable to pay the bill that such leadership would require, the United States seems to have little enthusiasm for assuming leadership in other military peacekeeping tasks and seems to be quite happy to turn Yugoslavia over to the European Community.

The conclusions which I believe can be drawn are as follows: Although the Gulf War proved the U.N.'s ability, under U.S. leadership, to turn back aggression, it provides no guarantee that a similar coalition would be available or able to meet any new threats on this scale in the future. Under domestic pressures the United States may consider it more appropriate, even when playing a leadership role, to be only "first among equals." A new world system must face these realities. On the other hand, it seems unlikely that a potential aggressor at the Iraqi level is likely to arise. In this case, and if the cooperation of many nations is sought, rather than relying on the efforts, resources, or direction of a few, the burden on any individual nation would be small. By approaching such threats multilaterally, seeking assistance from many nations, the difficulty in deterring minor aggression, and paying for the cost, will be minimized.

Ultimately, however, I believe that the only assurance that a new world system can be counted on to provide security and assistance in times of need is the existence of a sense of international community, a mind-set that derives from a natural, though sometimes latent, instinct to come to the assistance of others. Inis Claude, in *Power and International Relations* (1962) concludes that none of the traditional theoretical approaches to security among nations—Balance of Power, collective security, and world government—ensure effective management of power. I believe that we must therefore seek other approaches to world peace. If a solution cannot be found through the management of power from above, we must seek a balance inspired from below—through international community. Before discussing this idea in more detail, I present in the next chapter varying current perspectives on a new world system.

Recent Comments on a New World System

What are the forces at work in today's world of changing international relationships and new agendas? Or, put differently, what is the character of the world that is emerging? Various terms have been used to describe what is happening: integration vs. fragmentation, democracy vs. totalitarianism, pluralism vs. unipolarity, unification vs. diversity. What seems apparent is that the opportunity to create a new world system has opened at a time when diversity is on the rise and presenting increasing challenges to the goal of unification. Diversity, however, is not necessarily opposed to unification. What is needed is a balance.

As different commentators have suggested, today's leaders must recognize that diversity is not only a fact of life but one that should be both protected and encouraged for its potential contribution toward a strong, unified world. The challenge is to manage the two forces in such a way that one enhances the other and, thus, both lead to world stability and peace.

Paul H. Nitze, in the spring 1991 issue of the *Aspen Quarterly*, calls for U.S. leadership in a combined effort with other nations to make the world, in essence, safe for diversity.

The central theme of U.S. policy should be the accommodation and protection of diversity within a general framework of required order. The aim would be a world climate in which a large array of political groupings can exist, each with its own individual, and perhaps eccentric, way. Supranational institutions should concurrently have the task of providing stability and forward movement on important global and regional issues, those transcending national or ethnic boundaries. In such a world, the United States, with first-class military potential, inherent political, economic, and cultural strengths, and no territorial or ideological ambitions, can play a unique role in bringing its latent power to the support of order and diversity among diffuse and varied groupings.

Why should we focus on diversity? One of the most important lessons of the past few years is the near-impossibility of erasing cultural ties, ethnic identities, and social practices, especially in a world in which communications and, thus, ideas cannot be suppressed. . . . This leads to the central element of my theme—among U.S. tasks of the future should be the accommodation of, and protection of, diversity.

But let me make clear the constraints on such a role. I am proposing active U.S. participation in cooperative efforts among varying groups of sovereign nations to deal constructively with common problems; I am not proposing retreating from the world stage. . . .

Rather it is a time for wise leadership to bring
the great American potential to bear so that the
many benefits promised by a free and diverse world
can be realized.

In a world where diversity has only been accentuated
by the end of the superpower rivalry and the freedom
attendant upon it, European unification should be
recognized as a potentially stabilizing influence and
encouraged as a valuable force for progress in the building
of an international community. In November 1990, at the
Conference on Security and Cooperation in Europe, a
declaration was agreed upon that endorsed such a
contribution by providing for a new level of relations
between the European Community and the United States
and Canada. The declaration, which enunciated the close
political, historical, cultural, and economic ties between
Europe and North America, made a mutual commitment
toward safeguarding peace and promoting market
principles, rejecting protectionism, and expanding the
multilateral trading system. It also provided for regular
consultations and meetings between specified officials and
for exchanges and joint projects in science, the arts,
research, business, ecology, and technology. It is to be
hoped that from such measures as these the resources of
the world, both tangible and intellectual, may come to be
integrated for the common good.
Integration, as John Lewis Gaddis writes in the
spring 1991 issue of *Foreign Affairs*, is one side of the
competition overtaking the former ideological competition
between totalitarianism and democracy. Integration vs.
fragmentation is now emerging as the primary tension of
the contemporary international environment. What is

meant by integration is unity through the breaking down of barriers that separate people and nations. This is being witnessed today with the European Community's increasing cooperation in many fields, which is leading to greater security, integration of ideas, and peace. Integration, aided powerfully by communications and by the growing economic interdependence of market economies in particular, could lead to a more democratic and peaceful world.

The danger we face today, Gaddis warns, lies in the forces of fragmentation—especially those deriving from nationalism—resurrecting old barriers and creating new ones. He cites protectionism in trade and religious and racial tensions as additional factors that must be guarded against if we are to take advantage of the Gulf War success to find a way of deterring aggression through collective action.

A similar concern about a pluralist world's potential fragmentation was voiced by Thomas Hughes in a 18 November 1990 address, "Pluralism and the Politics of Peace." Speaking of pluralism as something more fundamental than varied special interests, he stated that he "finds in pluralism's progeny something that sustains our values" as well as "something that violates them." The danger, he said, is due to "the reduction in the relative power of the government to deliver, and the rise in the power of pluralism to obstruct." As may be concluded from the brief excerpt of his speech provided below, a forceful goal or goals to replace the cause of anticommunism is now needed to bind and focus a world that might otherwise lose the strength of its diversity to dissension and fragmentation.

With the collapse of communism and the erosion of the nation-state generally, these subnational tensions are reviving, sometimes in primitive forms. They threaten to splinter their erstwhile allegiances and spill across borders in disruptive, even menacing, ways. Neither neighboring countries nor rudimentary world institutions have seriously anticipated this phenomenon, let alone prepared themselves to come to grips with it.

There is something primordial about all this worldwide provincialism, chauvinism, separatism, ethnicism and fundamentalism. People power has proved adept at leaping over governments, tumbling walls, collapsing political structures, punishing incumbents, and sending ideologies to the dustbin.

As long as the artificial incentive of anti-communism sustained us, we could afford to believe in the compatibility of all good things: Democracy, development, arms control, human rights, ethnicity, governance. We could minimize the significance of the haves and have-nots, of the wide gaps in culture, religion, tradition and living standards. This minimization helped us continue to believe in rules of general acceptability, consistency and cohesiveness.

Internal balances are breaking down. Old coalitions are disintegrating. The inherited intellectual capital of the Cold War era has been spent. It is clear that we face a new kind of contest between the politics of pluralism and the politics of peace. Nobody knows how to grapple with this contest intellectually or politically.

The service of peace in contemporary America lies in arresting the descent of pluralism into acrimony and antagonism, in striving to bring purposes and means into balance again, and, above all, in stimulating new thinking that can produce operationally useful perspectives.

Of paramount importance in any consideration of avoiding international fragmentation must be the issue of what roles are to be played by whom or, even more basically, how we are to arrive at common agreement on the framework of a new world system. Bruce Bassett and James Sutterlin, also writing in the spring 1991 issue of *Foreign Affairs*, suggest that although collective effort through the medium of the United Nations has been proven possible and effective, it cannot be viewed as a simple proposition, especially in the face of the polarization of military and economic strength. It is my own belief that the United Nations alone and as now conceived is not the whole answer, though a revitalized United Nations would be part of it.

The new world order envisioned by Presidents Bush and Gorbachev would be founded on the rule of law and on the principle of collective security. That principle necessarily entails the possibility of military enforcement measures by the United Nations. Twice in its history the Security Council has authorized such action. The first instance was in the Korean War in 1950; the second was in the Persian Gulf in 1990.

The credibility of U.N. action to repel aggression and restore international peace and security, as foreseen in the U.N. Charter, has been profoundly affected by the response to the Iraqi invasion of Kuwait. The Security Council showed itself capable of taking decisive action. Its ability to impose comprehensive sanctions and see them enforced was clearly demonstrated, even though the ultimate effectiveness of the sanctions was not adequately tested. . . .

The vast majority of governments represented in the United Nations are unrepresentative, and most are dominated by class or sectarian interests. The United States is a profoundly nationalistic society with deeply rooted unilateralist attitudes. It is scarcely imaginable that Washington would accept decisive U.N. influence on its own policymaking. It seems most unlikely that U.S. public opinion would accept further American military interventions involving fighting and casualties in the service of an international consensus the United States did not dominate. . . .

The unprecedented level of international cooperation achieved in the course of the Gulf crisis, and as a result of the end to Soviet obstructionism in the United Nations, has prompted the hope of more international cooperation in the future. On the other hand, changes in the character of relevant military power, and in its distribution, and the drastic discrepancies of wealth that exist and are growing between nations of "North" and "South," threaten to produce a more anarchical and competitive international order.

William Pfaff, in "Redefining World Power," *Foreign Affairs: America and the World*, further questions the willingness of other nations to accept a traditionally dominant U.S. role, regardless of the success of the U.S.-led coalition effort against the forces of Saddam Hussein. Even in this situation of compelling mutual interest, there was in fact resistance to the United States' traditional leadership role, just as there was dissatisfaction on the U.S. side over others' response to the crisis. Although the episode was in many ways a promising demonstration of international cooperation, it would be shortsighted to hold out this effort as a reliable formula for establishing a new world system.

There are those in Washington who see the American response to the Gulf crisis as the model for a new American program of global activism in support of democracy and in opposition to aggression, or as leading an international coalition to do this. Is such a plan serious? In theory, yes. The idea of a world unlocked from its Cold War polarization, where conflicts can be aired at the United Nations, and where the weight of international opinion can make itself felt, as over Kuwait, is an attractive one. The idea of the United States as coalition-builder and persuader of international opinion is attractive as well.

This, surely, is not in the long run a realistic expectation. There was much reluctance in Europe, not to mention in Japan—where a government crisis was provoked—to follow the United States into the Gulf. Americans complain that the Germans and Japanese have contributed little to the Gulf effort, and that the French have acted with considerable reserve. But the unspoken reply of the Europeans and the Japanese is that they did not ask the United States to do what it did, and they are distinctly nervous about the consequences of all of this. It seems unlikely to prove a successful model for the future of international cooperation.

While it seems apparent that existing institutions for multilateral cooperation and the familiar pattern of international role playing will be insufficient to the challenge of establishing a new world system, and that adjustment must be sought in both cases, it should not be taken as a given that the United States will or can ensure that a new world system is accomplished. First of all, success will come only through *cooperative* effort. Second, the United States faces significant internal problems, regardless of its being uniquely gifted to lead the world onto new ground.

Owen B. Butler, chairman of the board of trustees of the prestigious Committee for Economic Development, stated recently (as reported in "Saving our Schools," *Fortune Magazine*), "The United States is evolving into a new position in the world, a new type of international leader." He describes this role as being, in addition to the traditional role, "a beacon of democracy," one of a "catalyst for change, a rallier of nations." While giving other nations their due, he believes that "no other country can yet muster the combination of political, military, economic, and moral persuasion necessary for military leadership in the 21st century."

At the same time, however, Butler acknowledges the pressing need for the United States to get its own house in order if it is to fulfill its potential role.

> This new leadership role . . . is not a foregone conclusion. Our economy and society are plagued with problems—ranging from social welfare to education to federal budget management—that threaten to erode our competitiveness and stability. And all these conditions have fueled a growing sense that a U.S. decline from leadership status is inevitable.
>
> To be sure, there are many problems that must be addressed. But if we can come to terms with the

crisis in education, the budget and trade deficits, and other critical problems, our pluralistic, multi-ethnic, free-market society may actually put us at a distinct advantage in a world moving in much the same direction.

The United States can be the beacon and rallier, but only if we are clear about the strategies we will need to marshal this new kind of leadership.

Inis Claude, in an article entitled "The Gulf War and Prospects for World Order by Collective Security," takes the consideration of roles and institutions a step further and questions whether multilateral approaches can be expected to provide a guarantee of order. He expresses doubts about the reliability of any collective security system, coupled with doubts that either the U.N. charter or the League of Nations covenant was really intended to provide for collective security, although both documents were heavily influenced by this theory. By way of explanation, he states that any firm policy of punishing aggressors—no matter what the circumstances—is a hard line that confronts a wide variety of objections, beginning with a general "quasi-pacifism": extreme reluctance to use force, inspired by moral or prudential considerations or both.

Claude believes that the inherent weaknesses of a collective security system are such that the Gulf War episode does not presage the settlement of all acts of aggression by multilateral means. In addition to procedural and tactical problems, he cites the differences in views and interests among the enforcing states and the fact that a single approach means a delay in learning from and correcting failed strategies. Further, for success to be had, the most powerful nation must lead, and that nation may not wish to incur either the criticism or the sacrifices involved.

Claude concludes that there will be a "continuation of a consensus in favor of *selective anti-aggression*, entailing the authorization by the United Nations of collective pressure to be exercised by an *ad hoc* coalition under American leadership, and to include military means only if other means seem ineffective." He also quotes (Broder 1991, A25) Secretary of Defense Richard Cheney's remarks about the U.S. initiative in the Gulf War, a statement not contradicted by President Bush. "This happens to be one of those times when it is justified to . . . send American forces into combat to achieve important national objectives. But they are very rare. Just because we do it this once, it doesn't mean therefore that we should assume that we ought to fall back on it automatically as the easy answer to international problems in the future."

Henry Kissinger writes in the *Washington Post* on 3 December 1991 under the title, "What Kind of New World Order?" After quoting Bush and Wilson, he demolishes a straw man of "disinterestedness"–ignoring national interest–an approach I have not seen advocated. He then goes on to say that power will "be the nexus of political, military, and economic assets, through many emerging power centers." After properly eliminating world collective security, he advocates reliance on five major power centers, the United States, Europe, Japan, the successors to the U.S.S.R. and "probably" India. The problem in creating a new world system, however, is that only the United States has had experience in building the sort of system created to win World War II and the Cold War.

Kissinger pays only lip service to the extension of democracy as a means of achieving world order. He again creates straw men of extreme views: one disclaiming any further national interest to be achieved, and another equating U.S. interests to the furtherance of human rights, relying on the spread of democracy to "solve all other international problems." No one, of course, espouses a simplistic reliance on either of these extremes. Finally, Kissinger prescribes a U.S. global policy more regional in design, more discriminating than that of the Cold War, and less cataclysmic—one that defines the distinction between the essential and the desirable, and the possible against what is beyond our capabilities. He closes with: "Population, environment, and nuclear proliferation pose the most difficult problems."

CHAPTER FIVE

The Role of
International Community

I believe that an effective and lasting new world system can best be achieved over the long run by a continuing strengthening of the bonds of international community. What is international community? International community will never be a single political entity, or any one organization. It will be the net effect of many overlapping efforts by people and nations all over the world based on the willingness to cooperate with and assist others in endeavors for the common good. It is a mind-set, a secular ideology. A mind-set of community, in my view, cannot be imposed from above but arises as a natural instinct of humankind ascending from lower to higher levels. I believe we should accept as the goal for a new world system the fostering of this sense of community through example and education, through the creation of means of cooperation to practice it, and by providing the climate and conditions essential for its growth.

"Community" has its origin in the word *common* and refers to people who live in a particular place or region or who share a common organization or common interests. In a broader sense it connotes society at large. The term was

37

given specific application by medieval communes, groups of people living together under self-governing municipal institutions. In the 17th century the term *commonwealth* meant an organized political community, similar to the Romans' *civitas* or *res publica*, which connoted an association held together by law. Communism, on the other hand, deviates from this concept insofar as it involves dictatorial or minority rule and state ownership of the means of production, and tends toward equal distribution of wealth.

Community does not mean "One World," which is a catchphrase used by Wendell Willkie and long ago rejected. It does not mean world government. It accepts a world based on diversity and increasingly unified through loose confederations of equals. As I envision it, all nations would ultimately be involved, with due consideration given for their relative contributions, so as to create a new international order that would transcend the present East-West and North-South confrontations. Nations would develop increasing respect for one another and grow in their willingness to accommodate each other. Whatever past illusions may have bred complacency or lack of cooperation, the realization cannot now be avoided that all of us share this limited, overcrowded planet and must together work out our future here.

Looking at it realistically, we know that the world has not yet become a community, although it is believed to be tending increasingly in that direction. Many groups of people, cities and nations, including the United States and most other democracies, constitute communities. Groups of nations, led by the European Community, are approaching formation as a true community. Other political entities to which the word *community* cannot yet be applied may be considered to be only in the process of developing the sense of community; they might be termed a society of communities in formation.

No one with any knowledge of the effort required to build the communities in existence today would contest that the goal of a world international community is necessarily a long-term one. Creating even intermediate community groupings such as the European Community was a slow and painful process, as is evident from the years that Monet and Schuman of France, Adenauer of Germany, de Gasperi of Italy, and many others spent in developing the present European Community from the Treaty of Rome. U.S. diplomacy toward Europe during this period was directed toward this goal as well.

The creation of an international community will not come from a new organization, with a constitution and a bureaucracy of its own. Fundamentally, it requires changing *people*, not just governments and their leaders. The attitudes of government and society will evolve as do the attitudes of people. True community will come from those who have individually accepted a mind-set of community.

The efforts we face, therefore, require patience. They demand commitment and active responsibility. Cooperation means mutual effort, working together. Wealthy and powerful nations such as the United States must assist those less favored as they struggle toward improving their national lot; the primary responsibility for overcoming these nations' inherited problems must, however, be their own. They themselves must take charge of their future and be willing to make the necessary effort and sacrifices. An emerging community it must not be taken for granted, but must be cultivated.

The distinguished commentator, Zbigniew Brzezinski, writing under the subject "Toward a Community of the Developed Nations," in the Department of State Bulletin (13 May 1967), as a member of the Policy Planning Council, described very well the concept of community.

It is our fundamental belief that in our age we must seek to construct a world of cooperative communities. These communities need not be of one mold; there is no single prescription for them. Some may reflect similarities in development and in ways of life. Some may be regional; others may cut across regional boundaries. But the basic point is that today the profoundest problems we face are too great for the nation-state, the traditional unit of international affairs, to handle.

This does not mean that the nation-state has outlived its usefulness or that we seek to create a world of supranational political cartels. The nation-state will, for a very long time, remain the primary focus of civic loyalty, the basic source of historical and cultural diversity, and the prime force for mobilizing the individual's commitment.

However, today the world needs more than the nation-state to organize global peace, to promote global welfare, to diffuse globally the fruits of science and technology. All of these things can be done more effectively and more rationally if nation-states cooperate with one another in the setting of larger communities, of cooperative communities that reflect what unites them and submerge what has traditionally divided them.

It is to the promotion of such a world of cooperative communities that the United States is globally committed. That commitment is in keeping with broader historical trends.

How can we identify the difference between nations that are, or are not, guided by the spirit of international community? A member cares for and shares with other members; it does not try to impose its will but expects to negotiate differences and to compromise. International community imposes obligations of world task-sharing, and member states would be judged by the quality of their participation, which would determine the respect and rewards accorded them.

What would a true international community look like? The most important feature of the picture would be the absence of major wars, for democracies do not declare wars. Karl Deutsch, in *Political Community at the International Level* (1954), introduced the useful concept of a "security community" of nations who trust each other not to take aggressive actions. Any threats to world peace, then, would be from the occasional dictator who, like Saddam Hussein—the world equivalent of a bandit—ignored his global obligations. Resources saved from military purposes by the advent of international community would be available for the economic requirements of needy members, and for educational, health, and environmental gains for all.

Further, the international community would at all times exert a behavioral restraint on its members. It would make the pursuit of an egoistic or aggressive world policy on the part of even the great or near-great powers increasingly unpopular and difficult. Denial of human rights would result in community disfavor, justifying not just international ostracism but the application of sanctions or

even force. Arrogant, abusive, and threatening international declarations would come under the same restraints.
In addition, the growing moral strength of the international
community can be expected to have a dampening effect on
existing conflicts, backed up where appropriate by economic
sanctions or international forces under U.N. or some other
auspices. The social discipline already achieved within the
world's more advanced democratic societies would, under
international community, be set as the goal for attainment
by all states.

How do we encourage international community? A
broad-based analysis of all the obstacles that must be
overcome on behalf of international community is beyond
the scope of this book. There are, nevertheless, certain
elements that can be identified as critical to the success of
a movement toward international community. These I
present below. To obtain widespread cooperation among
nations and encourage a willingness to make the sacrifices
this will entail, a trust must be created that others will
respond in a similar manner.

A major impetus to the spread of international
community will be education. By teaching international
community, by writing about it, and by exposing the concept
through the media to audiences of all backgrounds and
ages, we will begin to change people, which is the heart of
the matter. We will begin to create a new belief in the
possibility that the nations of the world can cooperate and
live in unity. In bringing international community to the
attention of people, it will be to our advantage to strive for
specificity. The more detailed the coverage of actions that
exemplify individual or national spirit of international
community, and the more practical the suggestions that are
provided for putting this spirit into operation—especially at

the level of the individual—the more readily it will become a reality.

Perhaps the most direct way of inspiring trust is by action. The following excerpt from *National Interest and Global Goals* presents a compelling list of guidelines, a Code of National Good Conduct, which it is believed would enhance and spread international community. As a useful contrast, it describes those kinds of actions that inhibit cooperation.

Nations can further international cooperation by:

- Cooperating in international efforts to deter and contain aggression, aid other nations in distress, and fulfill other responsibilities as good world citizens;

- Furthering international trade, investment, and technical exchanges leading to increased worldwide economic development, employment, and improved living standards;

- Improving environmental, population, and health conditions, nationally and worldwide;

- Promoting educational, cultural, and other international person-to-person exchanges that enhance historical insights and work toward the development of a "worldwide cultural literacy";

- Encouraging increased understanding, tolerance, and exchange of views between the world's great religions to identify common beliefs that can form a basis for common action;

- Enlarging the scope of international media communications and removing restrictions that affect and limit their use;

- Enhancing the role of multilateralism through the United Nations and other international communities, such as the European Community;

- Accepting healthy nationalism as a basis for national pride and a spur to national development; and

- Seeking to improve the rhetoric of international political and intellectual leaders in such a way as to emphasize the constructive and unifying expressions.

Nations retard international cooperation by:

- Using unilateral force against other nations without first making a determined effort at conciliation through direct negotiation or U.N. peacekeeping;

- Giving for political benefit, or selling for profit, armaments not required for another country's reasonable national security;

- Engaging in protectionism in trade, investment, and technological exchange, particularly where this leads to the equivalent of "trade wars";

- Taking egoistic actions based on uncompromising ideologies, whether derived from nationalistic, political, economic, or religious motivations;

- Except in rare circumstances intruding upon other nations through covert operations, employing means not generally acceptable between sovereign nations; and

- Exhibiting attitudes of racism, ethnic superiority, or neocolonialism in relations with other nations.

Along with the idea of trust and cooperation must come a consideration of leadership. It should be remembered that leadership among nations is not achieved—even by the United States, as the world's greatest power—merely by claiming it. In attaining international community on the basis of equality for the common good (which is, I believe, the most promising approach), leadership will be bestowed on the nation perceived as willing and able to make the greatest contribution to the common good in particular situations.

How can we best expand the scope and quality of community among the nations of the world? Through the spread of democracy and human rights. A sense of community cannot be achieved without democracy and respect for human rights. These concepts constitute a triad and are so closely related that they cannot be dissociated. One cannot tell which is cause and which is effect. Community is the basic prerequisite for democracy, and vice versa.

Democracy, as we know it best, developed over the centuries in the United Kingdom and came to France through the revolution of 1789. It succeeded Napoleon's generals in Scandinavia but did not manifest itself in Germany (except briefly during the post-World War I Weimar Republic) and Japan until after World War II.

Spain and Portugal became democracies even later, only within the last few years, a circumstance that explains democracy's delay in Latin America. The Soviet Union has entered the beginnings of democracy only now, in June 1991, with its fair election of Boris Yeltsin as president of the Russian Republic and, more recently, by the formation of the first major opposition party under Eduard Shevardnadze.

The 1990-91 issue of the Freedom House publication *Political Rights and Civil Liberties* lists 165 independent nations, of which 65 are classified Free on the basis of civil rights and civil liberties, 50 are Partly Free, and 50 are Not Free. Twelve states in the Not Free category gained in 1991 over 1990. During the 18 years of the survey, the Free countries gained 7.23 percent, Partly Free 6.91 percent, and the Not Free lost 14.14 percent. Progress is being made. Free countries constituted 39.23 percent of the world's population, as compared with 32.86 percent for Not Free countries. Only one country, the Philippines, lost Free status.

The criteria provided by the U.N. Charter for democracy are: Rule of Law, Periodic Elections (one-party democracies included), Independent Judiciary, and Protection of Human Rights. Experts conclude that on this basis about half of the independent nations qualify.

Under the auspices of the United States government by Act of Congress, the National Democratic Institute for International Affairs helps strengthen democratic and pluralistic institutions in new and emerging democracies to create a more stable world environment. The institute assists in organization, communication, constituent contact, improvement of machinery of government systems, the review of electoral systems, and the monitoring of elections.

No effort is made to "force" democracies or impose "our way." In many areas improvement will come slowly.

There remain, however, many countries that have never known democracy and many so-called democracies that are not yet complete. India has, until recently, been a one-party democracy under the Nehru family and the Congress party. Religious schisms, overpopulation, and crushing islands of poverty pose serious problems to the furtherance of democracy there. Mexico is still a one-party democracy, which is popular but making little progress toward multiparty democracy. Although improvements have been made in Latin America, dictatorships have only recently been democratized in Argentina, Brazil, and Chile. And the division between the landowners and landless peasants has never been democratically bridged in many Latin countries.

Africa, writes David Alkman in *Time* (10 June 1991), has been influenced by issues of democratization and the change to mixed markets, but Zaire and Kenya face serious problems in overthrowing their dictatorships. He cites a resistance to democracy in the Arab world arising out of loyalty to hereditary monarchies, dictators, party regimes, ancient conflicts, and Islamic fundamentals.

Nevertheless, China is the only major nation where democracy has not made some inroads, with Iran a second. The democracies of the world now hold the major military strength of the world, with the U.S.S.R. hanging in the balance. This is a significant advantage to the emergence of international community. Although nondemocratic countries with a history of military threat—in particular, the U.S.S.R., China, Iran, Iraq, and Libya—bear close monitoring for the present, the world has achieved a new stability on which to base cooperation and progress over shared concerns.

How then can we form, enlarge, and strengthen communities from groupings of existing states? What more suitable solution can be found than that which has enabled separate groups of people with a history of political cooperation to live together in peace and harmony? This has best been done under federalism, or if conceived more as an alliance for international action, confederalism. Both constitute a mode of political organization that unites separate political entities in a way that allows each to maintain its own political integrity while sharing in the making and execution of common policies. Dispersed power centers, with their own governing institutions, safeguard individual and local liberties while permitting direct communications with higher authority.

I believe that world leaders should look increasingly to this model in the creation of ever larger groupings of states, on the way toward international community. This can also be facilitated by treaties for security, the creation of free trade or nuclear-free areas, or a variety of other multilateral devices.

While we recognize the many unifying forces in the world today, we must acknowledge that strong divisive forces also persist. By far the most serious divisive force in recent history has been East-West tension, that between the communist and free worlds. We should derive great hope from the fact that this has been overcome and strive toward developing further confidence between the United States and the Soviet Union as a part of the general preparation of international community. Ironically, however, we have lost the communist threat as a rallying point for free world cooperation. The world today needs new goals to take its place, and on which to unite.

A prime candidate for a shared goal must be the resolution of environmental problems, serious threats that directly confront us all. Many believe that cooperation in this area offers one of the best means of furthering a sense of community among nations. With this in mind, Frank Press, president of the National Academy of Science, has in *National Interest and Global Goals* made the following series of worthwhile recommendations for action by the United States:

- In cooperation with other nations organize an international effort of monitoring, modelling and forecasting environmental change to reduce the uncertainty in preparing for the future;

- Establish a focus at a high level in the U.S. government for coordinating all activities concerned with global environmental change;

- Evaluate Third World aid and development policies in preparation for environmental change and dislocation in the next century;

- Enlist the interest and concern of other national leaders in such forums as the economic summit, the superpower summit, and the United Nations; and

- Urge deeper cuts at an accelerated pace for chloro-fluorocarbons (CFCs) than called for in the provisions of the Montreal Protocol.

International organizations of all types will continue to play a valuable role by furthering the affairs of the international community, without derogation of national sovereignty. The most important, of course, is the United Nations and its specialized agencies, to which bodies not in existence may be added when needed. A revitalized United Nations should be considered the normal operational arm of the international community, which constitutes its conscience.

The United Nations cannot, however, accomplish all goals of an international community. These must in many cases rely on bilateral and multilateral contacts between nations, which can react quickly and avoid the bureaucratic handicaps experienced under any large organization. I would envision each nation creating a cabinet-level post responsible for community and U.N. affairs. What is needed is a highly developed network within and between nations, with one focal point, staffed by experts with the instinct for the role of international community in a new world system.

In addition to the United Nations there are countless other specialized worldwide organizations already furthering International Community, both private and governmental, and an equally diverse group of regional organizations, such as the Organization of American States, the British Commonwealth, the Association of Southeast Asian Nations, and the Organization of African Unity. The economic sinews of the world, ranging from the great multilateral corporations down to the smallest economic enterprise, also spread global community, as do universities, tourists, artists, athletes, scientists, and clergy. It is important that we recognize the contribution made by all these groups so that we may learn from their successes how to achieve greater international community.

For the goal of international community to be persuasive, people and nations will need the stimulation of examples of progress, and success. The world's democracies should take the lead in setting examples for community citizenship. If the United States and its fellow democracies will implement policies that take this goal into account, striving to further unity among nations and avoiding actions that are divisive, other nations will follow.

Further, those nations taking the lead should attempt to induce the spirit of community by enforcing its rules, where explicit, among the more reluctant nations. A measure that should be considered in support of this is the establishment of a process whereby the World Court or its equivalent would hear suits and issue judgments in cases where nations disregarded the accepted usages of the community. Ultimately, such decisions might form the basis for an international community common law.

Finally, cooperation among nations is most successful when it proceeds from agreement on desired results and a commonly accepted framework of action. For nations seeking to balance their own interests with international interests, this is of paramount importance. The most important feature of such an effort will be discussions and face-to-face meetings on the subject of a new world system. I suggest that consideration be given to a special world conference to discuss the potential of international community as a force in the interrelations of people and nations. An objective of such a meeting would be agreement on goals toward which the international community should strive, providing procedures and criteria by which to identify when a situation would justify intervention on behalf of the international community and how the burden of such intervention should be shared. It is to be hoped that such a world conference would lead to future regular and ad hoc meetings to increase understanding of how international community can be furthered and put into practice.

A review of present thinking regarding a new world system reveals no assurance that an effective plan can be developed along lines now being considered which can meet the expectations now being created. No conceptualization of such a system has yet been achieved. It is widely agreed that no plan can be based solely on the United Nations as it now stands. Neither can reliance be placed entirely on U.S. initiative or leadership in large undertakings, although the United States will, I am sure, always be willing to do its share and to accept leadership where required in large operations. Nor can reliance be placed on some new Balance of Power, which is an ephemeral goal.

The most promising hope that has been given here is the furthering and better organization of a sense of community, which is already widely held in cities, states, nations, and groups of nations. Although the instincts for helping and cooperating are limited in much of the world, in modern times we have seen tangible evidence of progress in the direction of organized community. Europe, which started two world wars, helped create NATO, the most effective system of mutual defense ever devised. The European Community itself attests to the power of international community, succeeding as an economic community and progressing toward financial and political community. Recent events in Eastern Europe have given Europeans a new basis for community from the Atlantic to the Urals through the Conference on Security and Cooperation in Europe. If to this can be added a new political union, or at least an economic union with the former republics of the disintegrating Soviet empire, most of the vast Eurasian continent will comprise two developing communities. At the same time most of the North American continent is being molded by the United States into a single economic community by the addition of a free market treaty with Mexico to the economic treaty already in effect with Canada.

International community has not yet been fully achieved, but it is not just a dream for tomorrow. It is presently being accomplished without derogation of sovereignty or diversity in the lives of cooperating members. Through confederation, treaties, bilateral and multilateral pacts, and private international arrangements of all types, always enlarging and overlapping, organized international community is being developed. A matrix is being created binding democratic nations together, creating an inexorable barrier to war and leading to greater cooperation in overcoming the severe problems the world now faces. This is, I believe, the ultimate concept of a new world system.

APPENDIXES

Comments on
International Community

In this appendix, I review chronologically the development of the concept of community by those who have given the most thought to this subject over the years. Throughout this development one theme stands out for its perceived importance, that is, the reality that a world community must take into consideration not only international interest but national interest. This is the essence of international community—nations undertaking self-reinforcing efforts based on incentives common to all people. Some commentators have taken pains to point out the potential complementarity of these interests. More recent analysts have gone a step further, suggesting that in some cases national interest can best be served, or only be served, through international cooperation.

Writing in 1919, T. J. Lawrence conveyed not only a proposal for a league of nations—in which all or most nations would be banded together to settle international disputes without war—but a strong appreciation for the role of national identity and national interest. His vision of a league, including all nations on a permanent basis, did not accept the notion of one world state. With regard to nations, Lawrence saw in such factors as "common blood, common language, common institutions, common religion, and a common way of looking at life and society" the potential "to create a bond between those who possess them much closer than any that unites them with the rest of the world." The maintenance of world peace, he believed, should be based on "The Society of Nations."

It was in fact such a concept that was embodied by the League of Nations, the organization so often associated with President Woodrow Wilson. Wilson's high-minded idealism was broadly appealing–to the American people, their wartime allies, and even to the defeated Germans. His aim was to liberate ethnic groups dominated by the Central Powers, assure that both the victors and the vanquished of the war were treated fairly, and prevent future wars through collective security.

The Fourteen Points that Wilson proposed, and that were accepted as the basis for the League of Nations and the Treaty of Versailles, were perhaps ahead of their time, perhaps lacking a degree of pragmatism that world realities still demanded. The League of Nations failed to keep Japan out of Manchuria in 1931, Mussolini out of Ethiopia in 1935, and Germany out of the Saar in 1935, and early on ceased to be an effective body. Yet the League was a step, and a necessary one in a long process, providing invaluable experience for the creation of the United Nations that would continue to advance the cause of world stability after World War II through to the present.

In 1943 Walter Lippmann, the leading U.S. political commentator of his era, focused attention on a more limited concept of community than that entertained by Wilson, a community in which one might expect and accept divergent and even conflicting interests. Yet to Lippmann, this competition was not a bar to nations' living as a community.

> The original geographic and historic connection across the Atlantic Ocean is not the frontier between Europe and the Americas. It is the inland sea of a community of nations allied with one another by geography, history, and vital necessity. The members of this community may not all love one another, and they have many conflicting interests. But that is true of any community except perhaps the community of saints. The test of whether a community exists is not whether we have learned to love our neighbors but whether, when put to the test, we find that we do act as neighbors.

Lippmann also, however, stressed the need to premise actions in support of community on their complementarity with national goals. "We must consider first and last the American national interest. If we do not, if we construct our foreign policy on some kind of abstract theory of our rights and duties, we shall build castles in the air."

Harold Nicolson, in considering the history of international relations (*Diplomacy*, 1950), linked the success of efforts by modern democracies to work out common solutions through negotiations to three factors in particular: "a growing sense of the community of nations," "an increasing appreciation of the importance of public opinion," and "the rapid increase in communications." This sense of community he described further as a movement "from the conception of exclusive national rights towards a conception of common international interests." The success of this movement he tied to the existence of a shared, compelling goal, a consideration addressed earlier in the present paper. The movement toward international community, in his words, "if it is to triumph over selfish or regional prejudices, requires the impulse of common external danger." It is to be hoped that such a threat is now less necessary.

Twelve years later, in 1962, Arnold Wolfers wrote in *Discord and Collaboration* about what differentiates national "possession goals" and the goals arising from the world environment in which nations operate.

> In directing its foreign policy toward the attainment of its possession goals, a nation is aiming at the enhancement or the preservation of one or more of the things to which it attaches value. . . . Because of the possessive nature of these goals, they are apt to be praised by some for being truly in the national interest, while condemned by others as indicating a reprehensible spirit of national selfishness or acquisitiveness.
>
> Milieu goals are of a different character. Nations pursuing them are out not to defend or increase possessions they hold to the exclusion of others, but aim instead at shaping conditions beyond their national boundaries. If it were not for the existence of such goals, peace could never become an objective of national policy. . . . Similarly, efforts to promote international law or to establish international organizations, undertaken consistently by many nations, are addressed to the milieu in which nations operate and indeed such efforts make sense

only if nations have reason to concern themselves
with things other than their own possessions.*

He goes on to refute the argument "that it is incompatible
with the essence of national statehood to devote efforts to
the creation of a 'better world for all to live in.'" "There is
nothing," he asserted, "in the functions the nation-state
performs to prevent it from engaging in acts of altruism if
its people or its rulers so desire and if in the judgment of
its leaders it can afford to do so."

Inis Claude, quoted earlier with respect to his doubts
about the potential effectiveness of a collective security
system, wrote in *Power and International Relations* (1962)
that the United Nations could in fact play an important
role. He conceived of this role not in terms of ensuring
military stability but in terms of transcending the Balance
of Power system altogether. The key, he suggested, was the
furtherance of a spirit of world community; the goal was to
meld diversity with accommodation and cooperation.

---

* Dean Acheson approved of such goals by the United States
"so as to maintain an environment favorable to our interests" (*A
Democrat Looks at His Party*, 1955). Paul H. Nitze adds that the
United States "can no longer look merely to its narrow
competitive interests within whatever structure happens, from
time to time, to exist as a result of the policy and will of others
or as a result of the chance operations of impersonal forces. If
this is so, it follows that a basic objective of U.S. foreign policy
is the creation and maintenance of a system of world order
within which U.S. interests and U.S. security can find their
satisfaction."

In its constructive operations in economic, social, humanitarian, and cultural fields, its promotion of the techniques of international cooperation and the spirit of international responsibility for the general welfare, and its furtherance of the tendency of statesmen to regard the problems of the world as challenges to be met by coordinated or combined action, the United Nations has the potentiality of contributing to the evolution of a global community which will be capable of sustaining higher forms of organization. The ultimate task is to convert the world into a pluralistic society marked by a high adjustment potential—by the existence of component parts which are susceptible of regulation in their relationships with each other and with the whole, through the processes of political accommodation.

In *The Third Try at World Order*, written in 1970, Harlan Cleveland describes a "fairness revolution" and proposes that the United States should commit itself to a course of cooperation, a course, he implies, that modern realities demand.

One key to the planetary bargaining process, a major element in our international relations during the years just ahead, will thus be the skill and sensitivity of Americans to deal with nations large and small on a basis of equality, dignity, and mutual respect.

There is a chance, then, for a growing sense of "world community" to underpin the third try. It's far from an odds-on bet; even if the attitudes evoked by ecology are already discernible, you cannot confidently extrapolate any curve that contains the human element.

But because the other option is a world-scale Lebanon, we have to wager that this sense of community—the consequence of the new conditions, the new awareness, the new power of fairness—will become strong enough to enable governments to get on with steps toward arms control, peacekeeping machinery, and good-faith bargaining about economic and technological cooperation to meet human needs.

The third try at world order will require much of Americans, because they happen (have chosen) to be citizens of the only nation that is truly global in its reach. But maybe we need this new adventure in "world order politics" as an instrument of American self-renewal—that is, to get our tall ship on a course that has history with it, not against it.

The question of whether the world was even capable of achieving "solidarity" or "global community" was the subject of the 1977 Ervin Laszlo report, *Goals for Mankind*. The apparent overarching finding of the report was that there was no such thing as an insuperable obstacle, no obstacle beyond the range of human capabilities to overcome. Furthermore, the study group held that there was no fundamental obstacle to prevent all nations from becoming members of the same world community if they did not violate basic human rights or attempt to force their view on others, a world community being a community that recognized the right to divergent national views. The existence of examples of marked advance in human concern and consciousness that could further "the world solidarity revolution" was accordingly noted.

The report specifically addressed the issue of security and held that there was no inherent reason why an international community could not achieve this major goal, or "precondition of human survival," through international agreements and guarantees administered on a global basis or through other trust-building measures. Nor did the report consider the existence of differing religious groups an impossible barrier to the forming of a world community; rather it identified this diversity as potentially one of its greatest assets.

In addition to the shared concern of security, there were other bases of common interest, the report suggested, that would be an asset in the development of an international community. "Economic security, steady and gainful employment, and access to the goods and services for survival" were given as dominant and universally shared concerns. To these were added basic humanitarian concerns, shared by all nations. A conclusion of the report was that to be able to draw on the unifying power of these interests, nations would need to avoid extremism at home and excessive ideological competition with one another.

Kenneth Thompson, in *American Moral and Political Leadership* (1984), cites the distinguished theologian Reinhold Niebuhr on a national approach to international relations involving assistance to less favored countries, an important aspect of the concept of international community.

How can Niebuhr's philosophy of "Christian realism" be applied to foreign policy? Self-interest on the part of the donor government plays a part in the motivation for giving aid. As a basis for aid this is proper. Indeed, given Niebuhr's analysis of group morality, it could not be otherwise. "No nation is good enough to do what is right, unless its sense of duty is compounded with its sense of survival," he writes. Furthermore, the principle of equality "allows and requires that the self insist upon its own rights and interests in competition with the rights and interests of the other." "No nation," asserts Niebuhr, "will ever sacrifice itself for another. . . . The finest task of achieving . . . justice . . . must be done by the realists who understand that nations are selfish and will be so till the end of history . . . but that none of us no matter how selfish we may be can be *only* selfish."

It is interesting to note how Joseph Nye, *Ethics and Foreign Policy* (1985), describes different attitudes held about one country's moral obligations to others. Total skeptics, he writes, deny any such duty on the grounds that survival and the maintenance of order must be stressed; just relations between nations involve self-discrimination, nonintervention, and treaty obligations. "Cosmopolitan" types perceive an obligation arising from a nation's responsibility for its actions as these will affect other nations internally. Those that Nye classes under "Samaritanism" would readily provide available assistance to another who is in dire need—even to the point that this entailed helping others at high cost to secure basic rights. If such distinct diversions can in fact be drawn between groups of people, then, I believe, we should take courage from this last group, for it is a spirit such as this that is changing the world for the better, bringing success and hope to places where skeptics never tread.

The opportunities are there if we have the skill and imagination to seize them. Almost everywhere we find a strong objective case for promoting the national interests of the United States and the general welfare of nations through cooperative action in international agencies.

These words were written by Richard Gardner in *The Case for Practical Nationalism* (1988). Far from seeing an international community as an idealized state of affairs, he considers that such cooperation is practical in the most compelling terms, and he urges the next president to "talk sense to the American people about the changed international realities that face them as they approach the third millennium." He further insists that "through his words and his actions, he [the president] will need to hammer home the essential message, now only dimly understood, that multilateral action can often serve America's enlightened self-interest by sharing economic burdens and political responsibility and by accomplishing tasks that the United States cannot perform as well by acting alone."

The American Academy, in 1989, produced a volume entitled *Adapting American Diplomacy to the Demands of the 1990's.* The academy concluded that the multilateral system as a whole is in a process of change, that it is adjusting to meet new global challenges. The essence of this change, moreover, is realism—based on a growing recognition of the need for and the potential benefits of cooperation.

Within the United Nations, a new realism appears to be replacing the politicizing rhetoric and posturing that has often impeded the effectiveness even of technical agencies. The Soviet Union seems to be taking a new look at the U.N. as an institution for constructive cooperation on world issues rather than a theater for propaganda. Unusual great power cooperation is reflected in the informal and collegial "living room sessions" among the five permanent Security Council members, which have played an important role in winding down the Iran-Iraq war. Third world nations also appear more pragmatic in their attitudes and expectations.

John Gardner's penetrating analysis, *On Leadership* (1989), highlights that a sense of community must be nurtured, as well as the importance of doing so. Gardner provides two examples of situations in which the sense of community broke down: during the Renaissance, along with the breakdown of traditional belief systems and social groups, and as a consequence of the 19th century migration to America by peasants whose lives had formerly been characterized, in European village life, by coherence, continuity, allegiance, and the experience of being needed. He points out that American leaders rebuilt communities by restoring a sense of shared values and social coherence so that members could regain confidence in their ability to influence the future of their lives and that of the community. A modern community, Gardner persists, must "be pluralistic and adoptive, fostering individual freedom and responsibility within a framework of group obligation." He further argues the need for each nation to rebuild its shared culture continuously within the changing framework of the expanded heterogeneous modern society. Conditions that he believes help give reality to communities are: wholeness incorporating diversity, a shared culture, good internal communications, trust and teamwork, group maintenance and government, participation and the sharing of leadership tasks, development of young people, and connections with the outside world.

To conclude, a sense of community is, I believe, so basic, widespread, and enduring a concept that it must be, if anything is, linked to whether there is some pervading purpose to be fulfilled both by the individual and the world. Such a purpose can, I believe, be seen in the geological and historical record. Of all the positive evidences of purpose, education must be considered among the most important. Knowledge passed on to others can help in the achievement of all other goals. If the chain of the passing of knowledge to younger generations is not broken, there is a cumulative endowment to man of all preceding additions to knowledge, enhancing man's apparently unique ability to help achieve the purpose for all being—including progress toward an international community.

Community implies both service and continuity—the gradual betterment of the human race. In learning how to live as a community we may not only fulfill ourselves but ensure that those who come after us enjoy the peace and freedom in which to do so.

National Interests and International Goals

On 1 December 1988, as the new Bush administration was preparing to assume office, the Miller Center of Public Affairs at the University of Virginia and the School of Foreign Service of Georgetown University invited some experts, listed below, to present papers and discuss an important problem to be faced—the relationship between U.S. national interests and global, or international, goals. Since this is one of the most important issues to be faced in creating a new world system, a summary of the meeting's results is reproduced for this volume. It reaches the conclusion that although national interests must be paramount, they and international goals are not necessarily in conflict but are complementary in that success for each depends on the other.

Contributors and Participants

Contributors

PROFESSOR LINCOLN BLOOMFIELD (paper only), Professor of International Relations at Massachusetts Institute of Technology.

PROFESSOR INIS CLAUDE, Edward Stettinius Professor Emeritus of International Relations at the University of Virginia.

THE HONORABLE HARLAN CLEVELAND, former Ambassador to NATO and Director Emeritus of the Hubert Humphrey Institute, University of Minnesota.

PROFESSOR W. DAVID CLINTON, III, Research Scholar, Miller Center of Public Affairs, the University of Virginia, and Tulane University political scientist.

DR. ALLAN E. GOODMAN, Professor of International Relations at the School of Foreign Service, Georgetown University.

PROFESSOR NORMAN GRAEBNER, Randolph P. Compton Professor of Public Affairs, Miller Center of Public Affairs, the University of Virginia.

REV. THEODORE M. HESBURGH, C.S.C. (paper only), President Emeritus, University of Notre Dame.

DEAN PETER F. KROGH, School of Foreign Service, Georgetown University.

THE HONORABLE CHARLES McC. MATHIAS (paper only), former Senator from Maryland.

THE HONORABLE GEORGE C. McGHEE, former Ambassador and Under Secretary for Political Affairs.

MR. ROBERT J. MYERS (paper only), President, Carnegie Council on Ethics and International Relations, New York City.

THE HONORABLE DAVID D. NEWSOM, former Ambassador and Under Secretary for Political Affairs.

THE HONORABLE CHARLES H. PERCY, former Senator from Illinois.

DR. FRANK PRESS, President, National Academy of Science and Science Adviser to President Jimmy Carter.

PROFESSOR ELSPETH ROSTOW, Stiles Professor of American Studies and Government, University of Texas at Austin.

GENERAL GEORGE M. SEIGNIOUS, II, President, Atlantic Council.

SOEDJATMOKO, former Indonesian Ambassador to the United States.

PROFESSOR KENNETH W. THOMPSON, Director, Miller Center of Public Affairs, the University of Virginia.

Other Participants

DR. MADELEINE ALBRIGHT, Professor of International Relations, School of Foreign Service, Georgetown University.

DR. JOHN P. GUTTENBERG, JR., President, Guttenberg and Co., Washington.

THE HONORABLE SOL M. LINOWITZ, Attorney, former Ambassador (negotiated Panama Canal Treaty).

71

THE HONORABLE JOSEPH J. SISCO, former Ambassador and Under Secretary for Political Affairs and President, American University.

THE HONORABLE JOHN TUTHILL, former Ambassador to the Common Market.

MR. EDWIN M. YODER, Journalist and Syndicated Columnist.

Each writer was asked to consider, among other questions, what were termed international (or global) goals, which were defined as objectives shared by other nations—as distinct from goals purely in the U.S. national interest. Such a concept is directly related to the future of the international cooperation and leadership that is currently evolving. American leaders must ask themselves: If the world is becoming increasingly interrelated, what common international goals should guide it, how will these goals be defined and carried out, and what role can the United States play in providing leadership? The following is a summary of the views and recommendations of the participants expressed in their papers and in the discussions that took place on 1 December.

The principals asked the question of whether or not, realistically, the U.S. public—and therefore its elected officials—would accept international goals that are directed to the benefit of other nations but might not provide direct, short-term benefits to the United States. Even though the concept of international goals carries with it an aura of idealism, would the average citizen accept the larger perspective if there was a price tag, or if such goals appeared to conflict with purely national interests? Dean Krogh poses the question: Are global and national goals two sides of the same coin? Do they compete, or do they run on separate but parallel tracks?

There emerged from the discussion a consensus. There was general agreement that new international goals are required to meet the challenges of the 1990s, but they must be grounded in a clear-eyed view of U.S. national interest. The foremost priority facing American policy-makers is to work towards a possible safe winding down of Cold War tension–towards peace with freedom– thus reducing both the threat of nuclear war and the costs now associated with defense.

At the same time we must face with no less determination U.S. problems related to what are termed the "Four E's": the U.S. economy, education, environment, and energy sources. In each case these problems pointed directly to the fact that until certain weaknesses in the U.S. economy are overcome, the United States will be limited in its ability to provide international leadership. The need for higher standards with a greater international dimension to our educational system arises from competition with other nations resulting from increasing world interdependence. International environmental and energy issues as well as population growth, are crying out for improved international cooperation.

With the underlying belief that these important issues are becoming more and more internationalized, participants sought to delineate ways that the United States could enhance its domestic interests by furthering international cooperation. The major world power centers and a group of emerging potential major powers, are moving closer together. Their domestic policies are increasingly dependent upon success at the international level. Each nation becomes more dependent upon having outward looking policies and a willingness to pursue constructive engagement across national lines. As a result more policies are carried out in the international arena. This new situation does not so much change the objectives of policy as it adds to the agenda, emphasizing more than ever the international dimension of policy.

Peace with Freedom

In one of the essays presented in this volume, General George M. Seignious, II, president of the Atlantic Council, discusses his recent trip to the Soviet Union, along with General Andrew Goodpaster, former NATO commander, and General Brent Scowcroft, national security adviser to the Bush administration. Seignious highlights the progress he observed toward reduced world tensions and steps being taken toward furthering world peace. Speaking of tensions and changing relationships between the United States and the U.S.S.R., he says:

> A decisive clash or a war between these two nations could quickly escalate to nuclear war, with high risks that extend to the possible extinction of the whole of the civilized world—a risk so catastrophic that in itself it creates a common goal for both the Soviet Union and the United States— survival. However, it is the difference between the goal of mutual and global survival and the perceived political advantage that could accrue through political intimidation with military forces that causes a high-risk situation.
>
> Arms and armaments, however, are not the real source of the danger and the tension, but are rather

the manifestation of strongly opposed political philosophies, doctrines, and goals. If this is true, it would suggest the need for a policy with two tracks. The first track seeks to promote a common recognition that political constraints on international behavior are a desirable first step in a national policy based on stable security as a primary goal in international relations. Coupling that goal with the second part of the two-track policy requires that a balance of nuclear and conventional arms be reached at a level of force structure that denies each side the capability to gain victory or advantage by surprise attack, whether with conventional or with nuclear forces. In such a two-track policy framework, a stable deterrent at much lower levels may be a realistic goal achievable by the turn of the century—depending, of course, on Soviet willingness to seek the same goal.

In my judgment, it is idle thinking to believe that total elimination of any major component of the force structure, either nuclear or conventional, is obtainable in this century. Nevertheless, a new dimension has been added to the global agenda from the policy changes that are beginning to emanate from Moscow. It if it credible—as I do believe it is—that a new form and texture of relations may be evolving and that the post-war/Cold War period in East-West relations may now be receding, it would then seem to be in our vital national and international interests to set global goals that would encourage what could be one of the watersheds in modern world history.

Analysis of the changes occurring in the Soviet Union leads Seignious and others to the conclusion that the West should neither prematurely alter its policies and strategies nor refuse to take Soviet policy changes seriously. "A responsive Western approach—based on a prudent and pragmatic analysis of the step-by-step implementation of [the new] Soviet positions—should be a global goal for the United States and its allies for the remainder of this century." This is not to imply that the Western nations should simply react to changes initiated by the Soviet Union; rather, "the West can creatively and flexibly set goals and policies that would move the world condition toward enhanced stability and improved relations," Seignious concludes.

Members of the Georgetown/Virginia group agreed that the changes in the Soviet Union require that the United States reconsider many of its rhetorical and policy constraints of the recent past. Another factor is that, within this decade, both the Soviet Union and China have changed course, adopting new strategies of economic development that are more consistent with the economies of the West. Both China and the U.S.S.R. have become aware of their need for technical and financial assistance from abroad and that this help requires, in turn, more responsible international behavior and a spirit of international cooperation. As 1989 unfolds, the time has come to determine the desirable dimensions we would like to see in a post-Cold War world.

At the same time, the United States is seeking to correct its own economic problems and enhance its economic competitiveness. While the successful pursuit of these objectives requires a delicate articulation of macroeconomic policies with other centers of economic power, it also requires a reduction in the cost of American military competition with the Soviet Union. In this case, as in others, the U.S. domestic agenda can only be successfully addressed in an international context, framed on one side by collaboration with friends and on the other by constructive engagement with potential foes.

All major powers are faced with the need for domestic reforms that demands a reduction of old ideological lines and historic animosities and rivalries. Such interaction requires in turn: peace, stability, and foreign policies less dominated by harsh rhetoric.

Economic and Educational Imperatives

The internationalization of the U.S. economy, which has already taken place, requires both increased multilateral cooperation and an outward looking attitude, and not only on the part of policymakers but of all strata of the population. The need to reduce the federal budget deficit is tied to the importance of improving America's ability to compete in the global marketplace. Political and financial leaders in other capitals worldwide are waiting impatiently for the United States to assume a more responsible international economic stance. Without a new approach the United States will continue a pattern of reliance on imported capital to cover our deficit and to finance our investment.

We desperately need to encourage savings. A recent report by the Council on Competitiveness states: "Our abysmal savings rate–the lowest of any industrialized nation–cripples our ability to finance productivity and growth, forces dependence on foreign capital, weakens our global competitiveness, and, ultimately, endangers our living standard."

Senator Charles Percy, former chairman of the Senate Foreign Relations Committee, points out a number of areas in which the United States requires urgent change. While graduate students from other countries are flocking to the United States, our own students are increasingly opting to seek high-paying jobs rather than further education. If its foreign students were to leave, one major U.S. university would have to close six of its graduate schools. By the turn of the century there will probably be one million foreign graduate students here. Meanwhile, many American high school students cannot locate principal countries on a world map and are reluctant to learn a foreign language.

American businessmen and U.S. diplomats lack facility for foreign languages, although some observers note an improvement in the languages and cross-cultural skills of young foreign service officers. Some firms do compete successfully, but many in the private sector do not think of fashioning their product and services in ways that will make them attractive to foreigners. Despite the enormous diversity of our populations, many Americans are geographically and culturally illiterate. This impedes U.S. ability to cooperate with other nations and to compete on the world market.

Similarly, many American corporations emphasize growth through mergers and takeovers rather than through increased productivity or through research and development, better engineering and marketing, and shrewdness. Many do not make investments for long-term growth, favoring instead those yielding short-term profits to satisfy stockholders. In many industries, wages and salaries are rising faster than productivity. In order to compete in an interdependent world economy, the United States needs innovative business methods and wholesale changes in national fiscal policy.

The general trend toward privatization of nationalized industry means that international corporations are, through their investment decisions, in a position to shape national economic destinies and international relations—independently of national priorities. Senator Percy points out the need for guidelines for the development of our national economy. He notes that, although we disagree with their approach and acknowledge that their economy is in disarray, the socialist U.S.S.R. at least has structured plans, such as their Five-Year economic plans. To many in the developing world, the Soviets appear to have answers to questions that seem only to arouse controversy in the West. While the United States is unlikely to begin adopting Five-Year plans, a new institution, the Washington-based U.S. International Cultural and Trade Center, was recently authorized by the Congress to coordinate agencies of government with international responsibilities, as well as cooperate with labor and industry.

In 1989, there can be no denying that the U.S. economy is "afloat" in the world economy and will sink or swim with it: There is no longer a water's edge. Former Senator Charles McC. Mathias, Jr., in a paper prepared for the Georgetown/Virginia group, also stresses the national economic dependence on other nations. American automobile manufacturers depend on foreign-made parts. The U.S. economy relies on the imports of strategic materials that are difficult to stockpile in quantities sufficient to avoid future shortages. Energy is another field where the United States remains dependent, and the lessons learned during the oil crisis of the late 1970s may soon have to be relearned.

Our defense industry is as dependent on foreign sources as others. We assume that our security is firmly in our hands, but it is clear that further efficiencies can, in many cases, only be achieved by cooperating with our allies in research and development as well as production, Mathias writes. The need to export is becoming ever more pressing; every American farmer who plants a seed is dependent on our government's ability to maintain access to markets overseas. The British Foreign Office is said to devote 50 percent of its energies to economic and commercial issues. The need to export is relatively new for Americans, but will grow and will require both adequate policies and a government able to negotiate successfully with other nations.

Relations between the United States and its allies in Western Europe have crucial security and economic underpinnings. In 1992, when national boundaries within the Common Market are scheduled to be erased for trade purposes, there will be serious political and social consequences. The people of Europe are already beginning to think and act like Europeans. When Europe becomes a more-than-equal trading partner rather than a gaggle of junior partners, European attitudes toward America will change. The terms of trade and competition with the United States will be altered. These changes will have to be accommodated within the Atlantic Alliance, which has been the keystone of U.S. security policy and requires a sound political foundation. Any perceptions of inequity within the alliance could cause sharp political reactions.

Global Dimensions and Environmental and Energy Issues

The composition of the earth's atmosphere is changing as rapidly as the course of international events. The increase of global gas and acid emissions, including chlorofluorocarbons (CFCs), is possibly the greatest threat to the future of the planet after nuclear war. The late Barbara Ward, writing in 1971, foresaw what many are still today incapable of perceiving. Writing of the impending environmental problem, she said: "The door of the future is opening onto a crisis more sudden, more global, more inescapable, more bewildering than any ever encountered by the human species." More recently, Norwegian Prime Minister Gro Harlem Brundtland declared: "For too long . . . we have been playing lethal games with vital life-support systems."

Today, experts say that for every one percent depletion in the concentration of ozone in the stratosphere, there is a 6 percent increase in the incidence of skin cancer. The evidence shows that CFCs are the principal cause of this depletion. The devastation of tropical rain forests and the use of fossil-fuels in developing countries are also threatening the planet. Environmental problems are not only a vital national priority, but one whose resolution can only be worked out in cooperation with other countries.

The 1987 Montreal Treaty limiting the production of CFCs, which now has the support of 50 nations, is an important example of the type of international actions that will have to be taken. Although the treaty may not go far enough, a significant result is the voluntary decision by the DuPont Company, the world's largest producer of CFCs, to cease production at a specific future date. Greater international leadership is required to reconcile the many different views of nations and private groups involved in environmental protection.

Is it not in the interest of U.S. farmers that the devastation of the Amazon cease? Yet Brazil and other countries seeking to compete in the industrialized world are quick to defend their right to convert forest to farms and exploit domestic energy sources. Wouldn't Americans have the same reaction? China, too, has vast coal reserves that are viewed as a much-needed energy source for economic development. But at what price to the environment? The drought of the summer of 1988, although possibly unrelated to the "greenhouse effect," increased the awareness of the American people that solving environmental problems involves sensitive negotiations with other countries. Many of these nations are at different stages of economic development and face pressing problems, and their leaders have aspirations that are similar to ours at an earlier stage in our development.

It now seems likely that taking steps to protect the atmosphere will be considerably more expensive, in the short run, than continuing along current lines. Alternatives will have to be found for fossil-based fuels, substitutes developed for CFCs, and the turn toward deforestation reversed, and the costs will have to be shared by all nations on some rational basis.

David Newsom, former undersecretary of state for political affairs, emphasizes in his paper that the United States should not only make the solution of environmental problems a high priority on the domestic agenda, but should provide scientific and financial resources and international leadership for these tasks through cooperation and patient negotiations with other nations. We must prepare American representatives abroad to deal with this task. Our leaders must also prepare the American people for the sacrifices that will be necessary to fulfill international agreements to ensure better health worldwide. Unfortunately, this must be accomplished, not in an area of economic surplus such as existed after World War I, but while ever-increasing demands are being made on our own resources.

Frank Press, president of the National Academy of Sciences, also writes about the environment, pointing out that there are often direct conflicts between national interests and global good, arising out of the asymmetrical distribution of the world's wealth. An appraisal of international goals should not appear so idealistic as to be viewed as utopian, nor so pragmatic that it loses a certain emotional appeal. We should think in terms of limited and achievable first steps toward an international community and describe criteria for those specific projects that might fit and are politically and technically achievable. This could include the following, which are not very expensive: global health problems (AIDS, etc.); drugs; environmental and ecological issues; food and food distribution; space; accelerators; and hazard reduction.

National Vs. International Goals

These and other observations made during the Georgetown/Virginia seminar underlined the necessity for a rethinking and revamping of U.S. international goals to make them more responsive to a work in change. How can we shape these goals in such a way as to meet national requirements and at the same time advance international cooperation? Professor Elspeth Rostow points out the generally poor track record of national and international goals set in the past. The continuity implicit in the Bush government and the "overall mellowing of the international scene" may, however, provide opportunities for a new statement of U.S. global objectives. They must, first of all, be based on a sober reconsideration of U.S. national interest, with the safe winding down of the Cold War as its primary objective. We must harmonize regional and international goals and assist in devising an effective strategy for dealing with problems in the environmental, food, health, and technological fields. What is really needed to motivate us is something akin to the great foreign policy statements of the American past, Rostow writes.

Professor Kenneth W. Thompson echoes this suggestion, pointing out that pronouncements of goals by private groups often are not grounded "in the reality of important historical events and circumstances." We have to accept the fact that we can only operate within existing international systems. Despite its limitations, Thompson argues that the balance of power strategy was a force for peace and stability and should be maintained between the United States and the Soviet Union, and between the Northern and Southern hemispheres. He questions whether world government and the elimination of all nuclear weapons can be achieved. In the end, says Thompson, we must rely on a tension-reducing diplomacy based on the identification and accommodation of national interests. Global cooperation still depends fundamentally on "political settlements that reduce international tensions."

Professor Inis Claude adds: "If and when it comes to a choice between national interest and global goals, both the governments that act for states and the peoples that constitute them are likely to opt for the former." It may be that an either/or choice is not always required, however, for national interests and international goals are not necessarily in conflict. Their compatibility depends upon how national interests are perceived and what larger international objective is proposed. In today's world, international linkages have such importance that global conditions—economic, social, ecological, political, and military—bear heavily upon the welfare and security of every state. Some global goals, therefore, may be ranked as important national interests of the United States. For example, former Secretary of State George Shultz stated in 1983: "First, there will be no enduring economic prosperity for our country without economic growth in the Third World. Second, there will not be security and peace for our citizens without stability and peace in developing countries." Only when global goals are believed to be compatible with the national interest can they be expected to dominate foreign policy.

Dr. Robert J. Myers, president of the Carnegie Council on Ethics and International Relations of New York City, agrees. He sees no conclusive support for a double-tiered approach to international relations. Yet there is some empirical evidence that a national state can grow, or graft on, additional characteristics of international cooperation. Dr. Myers agrees that in the event of conflict, national interests will prevail. Yet, over time, some coalescing of national and international interests might occur. Short of that, duties beyond borders are more likely to be an afterthought than a deliberate policy; however, they may lead nations, great and small, to attach more value to the virtue of moral restraint. "National goals should and will continue to be pursued in foreign policy with the goal of accommodation where possible and confrontation where necessary. The statesmen will still struggle for the appropriate means for the desired end."

As a contribution toward clarifying the underlying issues raised in considering global goals, Professor David Clinton points out that it must first be determined "whose goals." Should they be the common needs or desires of individual human beings? They would in that case constitute only the lowest-common denominator of basic needs. Or should goals be based on the wishes of the majority of the "world-wide cosmopolitan community?" World environmental problems might best be approached through the latter approach. In the discussion it was pointed out that the nation-state has, in some respects, already been superseded. A broader community approach would have the advantage of increasing the contribution of diversity in the solution of world problems. Clinton, however, emphasizes the national interest as normally the best approach, through give-and-take negotiations between the heads of the some 160 governments of the world. This approach is consistent with our present system of international politics and has the advantage of resulting in goals being determined by those who must pay the cost.

Political scientists since World War II have also placed emphasis on what can be called international governance. What basis exists for political relationships between nation states—the entity traditionally responsible for government—and the other nations of the world? While the United States pursues national policies that protect its national interests, George McGhee, former undersecretary of state for political affairs, believes it must also, on a parallel or "second track," seek to improve the international climate, both for America's own benefit and that of other nations. We cannot simply wait for international problems to arise; rather we must engage with other nations in preventive actions, establish in advance the necessary procedures, and create the experience and atmosphere of mutual confidence that will be conducive to the success of negotiations when they arise.

The Role of Community

How best can America go about achieving the climate of cooperation among nations required to reach common objectives? McGhee believes that this can be done in the same way that cooperation has been achieved within many existing nations including our own—through what is often called "a sense of community." Community is a term applied somewhat ambiguously to those living together, belonging to one organization, or having common interests. Community represents an attitude based on concepts shared by all great world religions. A sense of community cannot be imposed from above, but must be self-generating at the human level, ascending to higher levels. Community rejects the "One World" catch-phrase, accepting a world based on diversity and unified through a loose working relationship of equals. All nations, with due consideration for their relative contributions, must ultimately be involved, creating an international order that goes beyond the present East-West and North-South confrontations.

Participating nations must increasingly have mutual respect for each other and a willingness to accept accommodation with each other. The extension of what begins as a relationship among people to the international level can only be a long-term goal. The resulting system would require from its members a capacity for political cooperation and self-restraint, but not necessarily the creation of a new organization with its own constitution and bureaucracy. Such a relationship can be developed only by a universally accepted mind-set of community that provides guidance at all levels within national and international institutions.

The American experience is an example of how harmony among peoples can be achieved under a system called federalism, which unites component entities with different characteristics in a way that allows each to maintain its own fundamental political integrity. The question was raised as to whether a federalist approach would have much relevance for the present world situation. Formal federal structures are not necessary between nations if they are willing to act, in their relationships with each other, as if a federation existed. Members share in the making and execution of decisions. Dispersed power centers with their own governing institutions can safeguard individual and local liberties while permitting direct communications between nations and between citizen and government.

Professor Inis Claude concludes that none of the traditional theoretical approaches to security among nations—balance of power, collective security, and world government—ensures effective management of power. We must, therefore, seek other approaches to world peace. If a solution cannot be found through the management of power from above, we must seek a balance of restraint inspired from below—through the world community.

The world may not yet have reached a point at which any single set of goals could be agreed upon by all; national interests can still be expected to prevail over international concerns. Yet there are unquestionably certain areas in which the universal interests of mankind converge, such as the desire for peace, economic development, and a healthy environment. These items also figure high on the agenda of the United States. Clear distinctions can no longer be made between our national goals and global interests; our global interests are, indeed, the vital interests of the United States. The same is true for most other nations. Agreements made on the basis of a convergence of national interests have proven historically to be the most durable and sustainable. It is, then, of the utmost importance to develop a set of international goals that can further these commonly held aspirations, in cooperation with the other nations of the world. Such goals will only be effective if they are chosen on some basis that will justify their acceptance, or at least acquiescence, by all of the nations involved.

In our efforts to be both practical and pragmatic in the search for global goals, there was a feeling within the group that we must not ignore the deep altruistic and idealistic strain in American thinking. Rev. Theodore M. Hesburgh, C.S.C., president emeritus, Notre Dame University and renowned humanitarian, would base America's global goals on the concerns of America as a nation "conceived in liberty, and dedicated to the proposition that all men are created equal and endowed by their Creator with certain inalienable rights, among which are life, liberty and the pursuit of happiness." Our continuing difficulties in making such words ring true even to our own countrymen should make us realists in attempting to export these ideals across a vast world, with all its differences in culture and religion and political, economic, and social conditions. Hesburgh writes: "Despite all the differences, we are all human beings, all yearning for peace, although always buffeted, here and there, by a long series of inane wars. We share a relatively small planet, divided in crazy quilt fashion by often bizarre national boundaries . . . in which governments struggle to attain and maintain an often narrow national identity that is expressed in pursuing simultaneously national and global concerns. In the name of national defense, nations, big and small, spend about a trillion dollars annually in armaments that thwart their more real and vital concern for improving the human condition of their citizens, millions of whom are sunk in an abyss of hunger and homelessness, ignorance and disease, unemployment, frustration and misery."

According to Father Hesburgh "the quest for peace in the nuclear age is *the agenda*." We have made progress domestically against racism, but education, employment, and housing remain key problems. America's global agenda should extend our ideas of equality of opportunity and a better quality of life to all our fellow humans. By cooperating with others to this end we increase our effectiveness, get to know each other better, and build respect.

International Leadership: America's Role

To what extent in our search for global goals should we look for leadership to the United Nations, which represents perhaps the closest the world has come to institutionalizing a world community? Harlan Cleveland, former U.S. ambassador to NATO, and Professor Lincoln Bloomfield, point out that despite its failings, the United

Nations has managed both to bring about crucial changes in the behavior of nation states and to bring them together to consider broad issues such as the environment and the need for shelter and water, which many governments had previously ignored. There have been more than a few violations of such accepted concepts as the norm of territorial integrity, the respect for diplomatic missions, the non-use and nonproliferation of nuclear weapons, international responsibility for helping refugees, and decolonization since the U.N. charter was ratified. Cleveland and Bloomfield point out that following the 1972 U.N. Conference on the Human Environment, over 70 nations established cabinet-level ministries for the environment, whereas before 1972 there had been none. U.N. agencies have also played a vital role in improving international health conditions.

There are a variety of institutions created for the purpose of managing the affairs of the world on a cooperative basis. The Organization of American States, the British Commonwealth, the Association of Southeast Asian Nations, and the Organization of African Unity are examples of such intergovernmental groupings. A network of economic interrelationships, ranging from great multinational corporations to small individual enterprises, is similarly involved. The international networks created by the media, universities, foundations, the tourist industry, artistic groups, athletes, scientists, and churches must also be recognized. Recently we have found that when the body necessary to focus on a specific issue does not exist, it can be created successfully on an ad hoc regional basis by the states directly involved.

There was considerable discussion by the Georgetown-Virginia group of leadership at the international level, particularly the American role. Professor Claude argued that there was too much talk about spontaneous international cooperation, as if this just happened in the absence of leadership being needed. He believed that a great deal of unilateral international leadership is already being provided and that more consideration should be given to the requirements for leadership in this field.

Dean Krogh maintained that there is no substitute for the leadership America has been supplying in the postwar period, but noted that there is increasing evidence of others resisting it. If we react negatively to opposition, prospects for enhancing international cooperation will diminish. If we accept the legitimacy of resistance and let other nations advance their views, we can still be an effective leader. Progress to this end requires a different modulation of our voice, a new identification of comparative advantage, and a clarification of who can bring what proposals to the table. However, the United States will still chair the selection process—there is no substitute.

Former Undersecretary for Political Affairs Joseph Sisco emphasized the diffusion of power we are now witnessing internationally. America has moved from atomic supremacy to a part of a nuclear equilibrium and from economic dominance to economic interdependence. The United States is still number one, but is "first among equals." This puts a premium on consultation and consensus making. In the 19th century, a sharp distinction could be made between domestic and international affairs. Today there is an inextricable link between the two. Their goals are near inseparable.

Professor Elspeth Rostow observed that although we have been dealing with a diffusion of power in the world for a generation, we have not acknowledged it. We have talked more of summitry than building a consensus, more about unilateral action than cooperation with others. We must be sensitive to the way history is moving. However, the United States still has an important role. As long as we continue to provide the necessary support for collective security, America need not be considered a country in decline but one which is in the process of organizing a new international relationship. The correlation of forces, as the Soviets use the term, has changed both for the U.S.S.R. and for the United States. The dynamic history of the United States and the dynamism evident in our present national resilience provide evidence with which to rebut any fatalistic assumption of American weakness, which is necessary if we are to play a useful role in the potentially promising but presently dangerous world arena.

Former Ambassador to the European Community John Tuthill observed that from the 1950s through the 1970s most Americans agreed that our international political objectives were worthwhile even in face of the severe immediate economic and financial difficulties. It would, however, in light of our present difficulties, be difficult to sell this argument to Congress and the people. Many in the United States, including the distinguished economist Martin Feldstein, oppose government coordination of international economic and financial matters.

The Georgetown/Virginia group agreed that short-term international goals adopted by the United States should not aim to change the internal structure of other nations, but rather to influence their external policies on the basis of goals that will further their interest and those of the world community as a whole. U.S. leaders need to pursue policies that give greater emphasis to consensus-making, to consultation, to working problems out on a multilateral basis, either within the United Nations or regional bodies. Although we have long-term goals which we hope can ultimately be achieved, such as furtherance of democracy, human rights, and a market economy, in the meantime the business of the world must go on.

The group found that it is not easy to describe precisely how the international leadership role can be played out. Leadership cannot be taken for granted or assumed; it must be awarded. A declining leadership role requires some painful adjustments. In many circumstances the United States has been asked to provide leadership, yet rarely have other countries wanted to be told what to do. The United States has been more inclined to speak than to listen; quicker to act than consult. The key to success lies in more frequent consultations on a wider range of issues—on a more inclusive, more institutionalized, and more equal basis. When hard decisions on international issues must be made, the world will continue to look to the United States. If we do not offer the example of a healthy society capable of responding to new problems, our capacity to lead others will certainly be eroded.

At home, our leaders must educate the American public regarding the necessity of a new thrust in foreign affairs. Many segments of our society are already aware of and active in such movements, and should be marshaled in a massive education effort, led from the highest reaches of government, to inform the American people and arouse their enthusiasm for a new era of international cooperation. In general, our postwar foreign policies, with strong public backing, have been worldwide in scope and have made a valuable contribution. We need not so much a revolution in foreign policy as an improvement, to adjust to the new realities and opportunities presented by the fluidity of our times. We need a higher level of a world perspective and effectiveness in the conduct of policy.

How can America best contribute to furthering the concept of international cooperation that emerged from the Georgetown/Virginia meeting? The authors of this Introduction believe that U.S. leadership can best be exercised not through pressure of exhortation but by setting an example through what might be called an "international code of conduct." We should choose policies which further international community and mutual confidence between nations (as given in Chapter 4). The achievement of a consensus on basic fundamentals for the conduct of international affairs would provide a strong beginning to a new era of international cooperation.

CONCLUSIONS

1. *The Centrality of United States Interests*

The primary objective of American foreign policy is to further our national security and interests. Since in the present world setting this increasingly involves other nations, U.S. national goals cannot be achieved without a further internationalization of our foreign relations. This will require an expansion in our multilateral relations, to assure the cooperation and assistance of other nations who can help us with our national problems. The high priority assigned to our own national interests is not entirely self-serving. It can also be justified on the basis of the general benefit to all nations of a strong U.S. economy, which enhances our role in collective security and international economic and technological progress.

2.   *The Pursuit of Parallel International Goals*

In addition to purely national goals we must also pursue, on what might be termed a parallel or "second track," international goals we share with other nations in order to avert conflicts and problems, and to improve the basis for international negotiations and cooperation. Our national and international goals will not always be identical; however, there need not be serious conflict. The American public and its elected leaders will serve as checks against international goals that conflict fundamentally with U.S. interests or entail excessive costs. The U.S. commitment to international goals need not necessarily involve massive new credits or resource transfers. Assistance from existing international institutions, combined with a further liberalization of trade and a restructuring and scaling down of private Third World debt, should be sufficient for most purposes. There appears to be no disposition on the part of the American public, or indeed other industrialized nations, to revive the massive aid programs of the immediate postwar period.

3.   *Improving the International Climate*

Improvement should also be sought in the general international climate through the development within and between nations of what could be called "a sense of community." The United States can best contribute to this by setting an example of good citizenship within the community, including acceptance of what might be called an international "code of conduct" for the community's members.

4. *Seizing the Opportunity to Assure a Secure Peace*

The United States must take advantage of the unusual opportunity offered by the present fluidity of the international situation and the growing sense of community, to seek help from other nations in solving or national problems. Emphasis must be placed on strengthening our national security, including making progress in resolving two related issues that seriously disrupt international relations, burden the world's economy, prevent the winding down of the "Cold War," and postpone the realization of a true international community: that is, the building of a basis of confidence between the Soviet Union and the United States, together with our Western allies, and continued major reductions in nuclear and conventional arms, which would constitute in itself a major step in this direction.

5. *Strengthening our Economy Through International Cooperation*

We must also, with equal emphasis, take strong measures to strengthen our national economy as a prerequisite to playing an appropriate role in international affairs. We must to this end utilize all of the assistance we can gain from others through, *inter alia*: improving our educational system by gaining access to the skilled personnel and technology of other nations; assurance of access to foreign supplies of scarce raw materials and energy resources; cooperation in multinational manufacturing enterprises; and assistance by other nations in overcoming international environmental and population problems.

6. *America Must Fill the Present World Leadership Vacuum, But in a New Role*

America still exercises the major world leadership role since there is no one to succeed us. We must, however, adjust to a change from dominance to "first among equals." Superpower summitry must be complemented by consensus building; unilateral declarations and actions must be succeeded by working together with other nations. We must employ a different and more modulated voice and more realistic definitions of comparative advantage. While the United States will still sit in the head chair in international forums, the arrangement should be more orchestral. By moving in wider circles of world cooperation, our policies can gain greater support.

Arms Expenditures

In the U.S. Arms Control and Disarmament Agency's *World Military Expenditures and Arms Transfers, 1988* the global arms budget was given at an estimated $1 trillion, which may have represented a peak. Arms exports from all countries were given as $47 billion for 1987, down from a peak of $57 billion in 1984.

Total Industrial Employment from *Statistical Yearbook, 1985/86* (United Nations, 1988) gave Share of Industrial Work Force Employed in Military-Serving Industry, Selected Countries, Mid-Eighties. These were topped by Israel at 22.6 percent, and among the powers, the United States at 11 percent, China at 10 percent, the U.S.S.R. at 9.7 percent, and the United Kingdom at 9 percent.

The World Bank's *World Development Report of 1987* gave the following as the percentage of central government expenditures that involved defense expenditures for the years 1972 and 1985.

	1972	1985
China, India, and Other Low Income Countries	17.2	19.8
Lower Middle Income Countries	15.7	14.2
Middle Income Countries	14.4	11.0
Upper Middle Income Countries	14.4	9.7
High Income Oil Exporters	9.8	23.6
Industrial Market Economies	20.9	16.8

U.S.S.R. Non-reporting

It will be noted that percentage of military expenditures in all went down except for the high income oil exporters. In almost all countries expenditures for education in 1985 were less than those for defense. The highest percentages for defense expenditures in 1985 (those above 20 percent) were Yugoslavia, 54.8 percent; United Arab Republic, 45.3 percent; Oman, 43 percent; Pakistan, 32 percent; Yemen, 30.1 percent; Republic of Korea, 29.7 percent; Israel, 27.8 percent; Jordan, 27.7 percent; United States, 24.9 percent; El Salvador, 20.3 percent; Thailand, 20.2 percent; and Germany, 9.2 percent. There were no figures for the United Kingdom, France or Japan. Of Industrial Market Economies Reported, the United States was by far the highest.

The largest percentages of expenditures by the U.S.S.R. and members of NATO were based almost entirely on the Cold War. In the Middle East expenditures were based on possible conflict with Iran, Iraq, and Israel. In Latin America military expenditures were based principally on internal conflicts.

The New World Order*

GEORGE C. McGHEE

NARRATOR: During and following the war in the Persian Gulf, President Bush referred on many occasions to our goal as the New World Order. Ambassador George McGhee has come today to tell us what a New World Order might be.

His story has been one of success both in the private and in the public sector. Following a Rhodes scholarship and a Ph.D. from Oxford University, he began his career as a registered professional engineer, a subsurface geologist for Atlantic Refining Company, and an independent explorer and oil producer. He was a partner in De Golyer, MacNaughton, and McGhee, and later the owner of McGhee Production Company. In these capacities he established a reputation throughout the private sector.

However, he also has served in the public sector as an official of the War Production Board and of the Combined Raw Materials Board. From 1947 to 1949, he was

---

Presented in a Forum at the Miller Center on 21 June 1991.

coordinator for aid to Greece and Turkey. He has held three ambassadorships—to the Federal Republic of Germany, to Turkey, and as ambassador-at-large. He was an assistant secretary and then undersecretary of state for political affairs.

Ambassador McGhee is the author of *Envoy to the Middle World*. He also is the catalyst who encouraged some of us at this table to participate in a project that led to the publication of *National Interest and Global Goals*.

It is a tribute to him and perhaps an index of interest in the subject that so many of you are joining Ambassador McGhee this morning.

AMBASSADOR McGHEE: I'm speaking to you today really as sort of a trial balloon on a new venture on which Ken and I have embarked. The question of the New World Order is widely discussed. This new project of ours is aimed at an end product which probably will be entitled *Toward a New World Order: World Community and National Diversity*. My own contribution will be mainly in the concept of world community, which I will discuss with you today.

What does *New World Order* mean? I think those of you who read the government releases, much like I, consider that it has not been very clearly defined. It speaks of peace and freedom, which probably it should, but is not very specific. Since the name itself isn't substantive, we have yet to define what the New World Order is. All we know is that it seems like a bold, innovative approach to our major world problems.

The best example we have of it is the action of the United Nations in putting together the coalition that under American leadership conceived, led, and won the Persian

Gulf War. This war was somewhat different from the other wars we have fought recently, and we have fought quite a few—more than most countries. The other wars—against Gadhafi, Noriega, and the communist dictator in Grenada—were all fought alone. They were rather small wars; we didn't need anyone else.

This one was a bigger war, and we fought it in concert with half the nations of the world, with 15 nations making a military contribution. Although we and other nations contributed more than others, it was truly an international effort under the United Nations in accordance with the provisions of the Charter of the United Nations.

Since that time there have been other actions which might help to define what *New World Order* means. When the Kurdish refugees seemed to be in danger, we hesitated for a moment, seemingly not knowing whether this was part of the New World Order; but with the impetus of the British and other Europeans, we wholeheartedly joined the relief effort and have shown that a threat to two million refugees also qualifies as action under our New World Order. We have also seen that the nations of the world responded very generously in Bangladesh when the cyclone swept that country, killing 200,000 people. Everyone seemed to agree that the New World Order also comprised helping people in such distress.

Where else does it go? In a sense, that is what is being discussed now more than almost anything else. If you read *Foreign Affairs* or the Sunday supplements to the newspapers, you see many articles about what the New World Order means. I might just mention a few I have seen.

Tom Hughes, the head of the Carnegie Foundation, recently took a very gloomy view of our current world situation. He called it a pluralist explosion of strong, divergent forces. He found no solution to the problem but seemed to think that we must grapple with these problems of pluralism and peace in an intellectual way and come up with something politically innovative as a solution.

Paul Nitze, writing recently in the *Aspen Quarterly*, analyzes the basic problem as being the "accommodation and protection of diversity in the world within a general framework of required order." In *Foreign Affairs*, John Gaddis describes the problem that we face today as replacing the competition between the totalitarian forces of the world and democracy, which we have won, with one between integration and fragmentation in the contemporary world. He finds both of these forces, arguing that if either one were to get out of line with the other, there will either be world anarchy or dictatorial rule. Gaddis advocates a balance between these two forces of fragmentation and integration.

The writer Charles Krauthammer has recently proposed a unipolar solution to the problem. This is rather a U.S. nationalistic proposal. We are to be the main motivator, taking the lead that the world will follow, since we obviously are the only remaining superpower. This is not by choice but due to the default of our only competitor, the U.S.S.R.

On the other hand, Jeane Kirkpatrick says that we must take advantage of our Persian Gulf victory to give up the dubious benefits of superpower status and the unusual burdens it might entail, and to return to more normal times, such as taking care of our own country. George Mitchell has said with great firmness that America is not ready to save the world or rule the world, that we have too many problems at home.

When we come to look at what world order might be, let us just speculate a little as to what it might be in addition to the United Nations meeting aggressive acts and putting the aggressor back in its place. We haven't yet decided, for example, to what extent we will become interested in the internal affairs of other countries. The United Nations has traditionally not intervened in such affairs. The United States normally has not either, although we did quite recently, perhaps as a part of a unipolar impetus. It appears to be an advantage in Ethiopia, where we have attempted to arbitrate between the government and the opposing forces overthrowing the communist regime; we decided in favor of the rebels and invited them into Addis Ababa. The people of Addis Ababa didn't particularly like that; the revolutionaries were largely controlled by Eritreans who mainly seek their own independence. In the end, however, I think the peace was saved. Is this indicative of the type of unipolar actions which we might in the future get ourselves involved in?

We might also find other problems. What about countries in which genocide has been occurring on a large scale, like the Sudan? What about situations like that in Liberia, where three would-be dictators fought to the death amid destruction of their country, with no outside intervention by the Western powers? Only a small force from ECOWAS (Economic Community of West African States) attempted to solve this debacle. And yet, the United States created Liberia originally. A lot of people, including the Liberians, thought we should have done something by intervening. Under the New World Order, would we intervene in such a situation?

Would we intervene, for example, in Yugoslavia, where there has been bloodshed on behalf of Slovenian independence? What do we do, for example, about mass movements of people from the overpopulated areas of the world? We hear today about airplanes coming from China by various routes and dumping a couple of hundred people who paid $50 or $100 a piece to plant them in America. Suppose the Chinese and the Indians of South Asia have the opportunity to pay $100 to a man with a big boat who dumps them on the shore of South Carolina. The Poles are expecting about a million Russians to force their way into their country if the Soviet Union breaks up as it appears it might.

Marginal threats, threats that could or could not be important enough to involve the New World Order, might be considered on a case-by-case basis. Perhaps we could eventually develop some rules like those of British common law, which would decide which case is worth the intervention of the international community. Perhaps in time we can develop techniques more forceful than those that we used before the fighting in the Persian Gulf, for putting pressure on countries who have violated the international community's rights. We have many tools at our disposal: the threat of seizure of their foreign exchange abroad; the stoppage of entry into their country of all naval vessels and aircraft; the stopping of telecommunications with them; and the boycotting of their exports and the banning of food, armaments, and other imports. By adding the force of all of these sanctions, it might be possible to put enough pressure on a country in violation of the rules of the New World Order to relent and capitulate.

We had a very good embargo working against Saddam Hussein, and it is perhaps a little disappointing that we didn't get to see whether it would have worked, particularly because it is the first time that a blockade of that magnitude has ever been created. There were many people who thought it had an outside chance of bringing Saddam Hussein to heel. If the ground war had never taken place, if the Iraqi central government could have been pressured to withdraw their troops to get the blockade released, think of the savings in loss of life and treasure and political disunity which was created by the ground war. This is not to deprecate the war—it was very successful, and we owe a great deal to those who participated. It succeeded in freeing Kuwait, but it left a great many problems in its wake that would never have existed if we had developed a type of coercion which could force capitulation. Eisenhower is quoted as saying that you can never predict how war is going to turn out.

Now let me tell you a little about my own approach to the New World Order through the concept of world community. World community is not intended to be world government. If you read the books on this subject, you will find that the concept of world community assumes diversity, as Paul Nitze recently emphasized in *Foreign Affairs*. In a sense, the world must be made safe for diversity—the perpetuation of the rights of nations for diversity in their ways of life is very important and is worth saving.

Looking at it very broadly, my concept of world community is an attitude of mind towards the relations between individuals and states, based in essence on the principle of the Golden Rule, which is a part of every world religion and which stems from instincts very deep in men. In a sense, I propose that we attack world peace through ordinary people and their attitudes toward each other, as being more powerful than the roles of political parties, and leaders of states.

You can't impose a feeling of community by authority from above. In my view, it is a self-generating attitude by man which ascends from lower to higher levels. Going beyond the present classifications of North-South and East-West, all nations must become involved, with due consideration given to their relative strength, if world community is to have the ultimate effect we would hope for it. Increasingly, these countries must have more mutual respect for each other—an increased willingness to accept accommodation with each other. No matter what illusions we have held for the future, the people in this limited, troublesome planet Earth must work together to solve our problems.

The word *community* has its origin in the word *common*. *Community* is used in referring to people who live in a particular place or who share a common organization or a common interest. In a broader sense, it connotes society at large. The term has had specific applications in the designation of medieval communes, as groups of people living together under self-governing municipal institutions. In the 17th century the term *commonwealth* meant an organized political community, like the Roman words *civitas* or *res publica*, which connoted an association held together by law.

Communism, on the other hand, has a sharply contrasting meaning, because we know that it involves dictatorial or at best minority rule. We know that it also includes state ownership of the means of production and tends towards equal distribution of wealth. None of this is inherent in the concept of community. Community has no ideological base; community flows from the deepest instincts of men.

How do you get people to live and work together in a community? You have an example here in Charlottesville. The fact that such a representative group is here today is a part of your feeling of community here. We have a feeling of community as a nation, and this is shared by most civilized countries of the world. I lived for three years in England, and the main thing that impressed me about England was the deep feeling of community that people had, from the smallest village to the county to the nation. It is something you don't have to define; everyone understands what it means. Everyone knows it means the capacity for working together.

This is a long-term goal. It won't come with some new, fancy organization, a constitution, or a bureaucracy of its own. It will come only when people have the mind-set of community that governs when any situation involving the community or a threat to the community arises. We need to change people so that they will automatically react in that way, no matter where they are in society—from the president down to the person at the lowest economic level. In this way we will act as a community, as a whole.

There are lots of organizations that have been created in the world which carry out this feeling. Churches do; professional organizations do. A university has a community feeling. People engaged in common sporting activities have a community feeling, and it is that aggregate of all of these which, becoming stronger in the face of broader and more serious problems, will provide the answer to our problem.

How can you identify a nation that doesn't share this view, that doesn't act like a member of the community? You can tell by their actions vis-à-vis the other countries. Do they try to impose their will on others? Are they willing to negotiate their differences with others? Are they, for example, threatening in their reference to others? Do they still carry a colonialist attitude of racist superiority? How do they act in their relations with their neighbors? Are they arming unnecessarily? It is very easy to identify these things, and I will, as I close, give what you might call a code of behavior for those nations who are supportive of the concept of community and those who are destructive of it.

A proper world community will at all times enforce a behavioral restraint on its members. Denial of human rights would result in community disfavor, justifying not just international ostracism and rebuke, but the application of sanctions or even force if it is necessary, as in the Persian Gulf War. Arrogant, abusive, and threatening international declarations would come under the same restraint. People who acted in this way would not be accepted as a full member and given the rights of the community.

The social discipline that we find within states such as our own country and Western Europe shows how community could spread through the world, creating worldwide the same relationships that we find within smaller communities.

Apart from whether you share my emphasis on the importance of this concept, how would you go about achieving world community? What can we do to achieve it? Nations with wealth and power like ours must set the example by restraining ourselves. We must be willing to assist the less favored, and they in turn must exercise patience in overcoming the problems which they have inherited and which can't be solved overnight. In the final analysis, each nation must assume responsibility for its own future and be willing to make the necessary effort.

However, they can't accomplish this without help from others. Are we willing to give that help?

Let me read to you, for example, a few things that nations can do to further the concept of community. These are obvious; these are things that are in everyone's hopes and plans for the future. These things make it easier for people to live in a world community:

1. trying to increase international trade and investment and technical exchange so that there is worldwide economic development and improved living conditions;

2. helping to improve environmental, population, and health conditions, nationally and worldwide;

3. promoting educational, cultural, and international exchanges and permitting other people to learn the history and feelings of the countries which they visit and to find within them bases for common action;

4. increasing the scope of world communications media and making them absolutely free from state control, so that they can more easily convey the real attitudes of people in the world;

5. enhancing the role of multilateralism in dealing with problems, whether through the United Nations and its subsidiaries or through multilateral organizations created ad hoc to attack particular problems;

6. accepting a healthy nationalism as giving people the source of pride which makes them create a better nation, as long as this does not involve trade wars and impulses of nationalist origin

which create friction and animosity among people;

7. seeking to improve the rhetoric of international political and intellectual leaders in such a way as to emphasize constructive and unifying expressions, and not diatribes and accusations.

On the other hand, I think you can retard international cooperation and work against world community by using unilateral force against other nations without first making a determined effort at conciliation through direct negotiation or U.N. peacekeeping. I'm afraid that in recent decades this country has gotten a little too trigger-happy in resorting rather easily to unilateral and open political aggression and invasion, largely where we've found leaders whom we consider very bad and who we believe must be put in their place. European countries have not done this, and I think they have in general viewed with skepticism that we have chosen to do it.

People retard development and cooperation if they give or sell for political benefit or for profit armaments which are not required by other countries for their reasonable national security. A great effort is being made now to bring armaments under control. There have been times in history when they were under control. However, we've heard China say that she is not going to obey any rules and that she intends to export weapons of very serious purposes, such as missiles which can carry atomic warheads.

A nation undermines world community by engaging in protectionism in trade, investment, and technological exchange, particularly when this would lead to the equivalent of trade wars. World community is also threatened by egoistic actions based on uncompromising ideologies, whether they derive from nationalistic, political, or economic motivations.

Except in rare circumstances, intruding into other nations with the type of operational intelligence with which we and other nations have done, also damages the possibilities for world community. The United States overthrew the government of Mohammad Mossadegh in Iran. Although the shah returned, the Iranians have never forgotten that we admittedly overthrew Mossadegh, whom they considered to be the father of their country. They will not forget it in our lifetime.

Finally, cooperation in communities is further set back drastically when there is any evidence of racism, ethnic superiority, or neocolonialism in relations with the other nations.

How can we do something? I think by example. We are now the superpower of the world. If we would, not by speech but by example, act like a good citizen in the world community and attempt to abide by its requirements, this would have a great effect on other nations in getting them to emulate us in order to earn our approbation, as well as the approbation of other countries.

I don't believe that we can set out to be the leader of the world. Leadership is something that has to be bestowed upon us by others. We don't get it by being powerful or asserting ourselves as leader. We will be the leader only if the other nations of the world think we are the best citizen of the world community.

NARRATOR: We've asked Professor Inis Claude, who for many years has written, lectured, and thought about this subject, to make whatever comment he would like to make or raise whatever questions he wants to raise. Michael

113

Fowler, who is a graduate of both the government department and the Miller Center and also the Harvard Law School, and who taught a course this year in our government department, will also comment on Ambassador McGhee's presentation.

PROFESSOR CLAUDE: Ambassador McGhee has emphasized the idea and the ideal of world community as the objective for our striving, and obviously he is joined in this by a great many other thoughtful people over many years in holding forth on the ideal of a world community.

For some years now, I have been inclined to believe that a more modest aim is in order. I have come to believe that the term *community* implies an intimacy, a tightness of bonds, a degree of togetherness and unity, and a degree of integration that I think is neither possible nor necessary for the world as a whole. In short, I've come increasingly to believe that genuine community is essentially and necessarily a small group phenomenon, not a worldwide phenomenon.

I'm not at all confident that New York City is or can possibly become a community. If New York City is too big and too diverse to be a community, I am fairly certain that that is true of mankind, the world at large. New York City is not a community, but a congeries of communities in more or less tense relationship with each other. Unfortunately, communities in a city such as New York often have poor relations with each other. In short, I find it impossible to conceive of a global community. I just think the model doesn't fit.

As I look at states, realizing that sometimes they succeed and sometimes they don't succeed very well in maintaining stability and order and civility and a good life

114

for their people, it seems to me that states succeed—in so far as they do and when they do in these matters—not by creating one consolidated community, but by creating good relationships among the various communities that constitute their population. That is to say, I think a successful state is a society of communities. It has achieved reasonable social relations among the various communities that constitute the whole. I think I would be inclined to stake my goal for mankind, for the world at large, in those terms—a society of communities, a manageable pluralism, a world in which diversity works and creates something other than chaos.

Now that leaves open the very large and intriguing question of how we get there—how we achieve that. We don't even know a great deal about how and why it happens when it does happen domestically, and how and why it breaks down and stops happening domestically. We know that the United States did not achieve this happy situation before 1861. We know that the United States has been in that happy situation of a society of communities since 1865. But we don't have any very shrewd understanding of how some societies become successful societies of communities and others do not.

I think Ambassador McGhee and I agree pretty much on this despite the difference in terminology. He is inclined to use the word *community* where I would not, but he also emphasizes the point about pluralism and diversity in his remarks this morning. He has emphasized quite strongly the point that we are not talking about an integrated community for the world; we are talking about a pluralism of national communities.

I think both of us, in fact, despite the difference in terminology, do think of and continue to think of a

115

multistate system, but we hope one with necessary elements of tolerance, mutual respect, mutual aid, central management, and so forth, to make a tolerable world—in short, a kind of *e pluribus unum* ideal.

In thinking about how to get there, how to achieve that kind of world order, Ambassador McGhee endorses in a couple of places in his essay the approach of federalism. On page two, for instance, he talks about a world based on diversity and unified through a loose federation of equals. On the following page he raises the question,

> What more suitable solution can there be than that which has enabled people to live together in more restricted areas, like states? This has been best done under what we call federalism, a mode of political organization that unites separate political entities in a way that allows each to maintain its own political integrity while sharing in the making and execution of common policies.

I want to raise the question and would be happy if Ambassador McGhee would address the question of whether the general historical record of federalism in the world really recommends it as a means for management of a state system.

Mankind has a fair amount of experience with federalism. We have the notable example of the United States, which comes to everyone's mind immediately. We have the example of the Soviet Union, of Canada, of Yugoslavia, of India, and of Switzerland. This is not an exhaustive list. It is a mixed record: Some of these federations have worked rather well; others have not worked at all well.

We see that federations are sometimes plagued by civil war, by tension, and ultimately by dissolution in some cases. Sometimes they are marked by centralizing trends that break down the realities of federalism and tend to make for a unified or centralized state, ultimately, rather than the federalism that was initially conceived. Federalism is certainly not a stagnant, stable balance between unity and diversity, but is a constantly moving kind of equilibrium or disequilibrium between the two principles.

I'm not meaning to suggest that federalism is not worth trying. I would like to raise the question, though, of whether we ought to jump to the conclusion of the experience of mankind with federalism that this is the best approach, the more suitable approach, for dealing with the problems of putting this world together.

My own feeling is that before we've reached any such conclusion, we need to engage in a very extensive comparative study of the experiences of federations before we reach any final judgment on this. Why do they sometimes succeed? Why do they sometimes fail? What happens after people federate is a question that needs a great deal of exploration.

AMBASSADOR McGHEE: Inis and I have worked on peripheral subjects for many, many years, and I value very much his judgment. That is why I am very happy to discuss the points he has raised.

To take up Inis's two points: I have never thought of communities necessarily bringing dissimilar peoples into close personal and social contact. I have spent a little time in south India, and I had many talks with Mr. Nehru. I don't think I could ever really understand India. I hate to say that. I would be happy to live in a world where there

117

is cooperation between the Indian state and our state, but I wouldn't like to live in India.

The concept of community that I am now proposing is really a mind-set rather than an organization or ideology, a mind-set that governs the necessary relationships among people within and among communities at the world level.

The importance of diversity, which is in the title of the effort that we are undertaking and which Paul Nitze, for example, based his article on, is extremely important. The wealth of the culture of the civilization that is represented in Western Europe must be perpetuated. Hitler would have eliminated it in favor of his empire of a thousand years, but the cultures of Italy, France, and England must be nurtured and perpetuated, diverse as they may be, in the face of cooperation which must take place between their nations.

Certainly world government is the last concept that I would endorse, because I am not willing to turn over to anybody else the government of our country. I'm not sure that I would ever be willing to turn over to the federal government the complete government of our state. The word "federal" created quite a stir last week, if you recall, when someone put it in a document that is being drafted by the Common Market as expressing their ultimate goal.

I would think that federalism works quite well in our country. It is a very diverse country. I am not sure that we would like to live cheek by jowl with all the different peoples represented in the 50 states, but federalism is a loose binding which holds us all together while we continue to do the thing we have always done.

Federalism as represented in the Common Market is the best example, I think, of what it means internationally, and certainly what has been created in Europe is something that never existed before.

When I was serving as ambassador to Germany, I found the young people in Germany had much more nationalism for Europe as a whole than they had for Germany. They were a little embarrassed about calling themselves Germans. They were citizens of the European Community. They felt more at home knocking around in Spain and France and Italy than in their own country. The Germans today are the least nationalistic of all Europeans; they have adopted the concept of community within the Western European area.

I think you can see community developing in other areas. The Africans, for example, under the auspices of ECOWAS, got together and put 2,000 men in Liberia to try to save them from mass suicide. This is the first time that any group of states in Africa ever put together a military force to help one of their members in trouble.

The spread through the world of sympathy for people in the face of national disaster is an attribute of community. That is what we did in our communities here before we started doing it in Bangladesh.

I think the mind-set of community is a basic human instinct that is somehow related to whatever purpose living beings have in this world. My own experience, particularly as a geologist, leads me to conclude that there is a basic purpose, and I think it's tied in to the Golden Rule, or whatever you wish to call it, which is translatable into a mind-set of community.

MR. FOWLER: The first question I would ask Ambassador McGhee is this: What evidence is there that nations are gaining mutual respect for one another, and that nationalism, which many of us have seen as an inherently divisive and perhaps a revolutionary force, is now turning into a unifying force, a force that might cement ties among this emerging world community?

Second, in the past, have not political and national conflict regularly spilled over to hamper international cooperation, whether within the United Nations or otherwise?

AMBASSADOR McGHEE: That is a good question, and I think there is a clear answer. I think healthy nationalism is one of the most important forces in the world. Many of the things that we do in this community derive from national pride—pride as a Virginian, pride as an American. To disturb that, I think, would be a great loss.

On the other hand, we have seen the misuses of nationalism. Hitler took German degradation after the First World War and the presumed unfairness of the peace treaty and used that to inflame German nationalism to the point that they wished to conquer the world and conduct genocide on a massive scale. This, of course, is the obvious misuse of nationalism.

As I said, I think nationalism is being transferred before our eyes from European nations to the Common Market, or maybe to all of Europe to the Urals, which is the goal of Europeans generally. They all look to not just economic unity, which they have now, but political unity and maybe common citizenship. All this seems possible.

There are examples of hostility toward unity caused by nationalism. But where a balance can be achieved, utilizing the energies of the separate nationalisms for the benefit of a community of nations, such a federation is possible. One simply has to look very broadly at history; we have gone from a time of world anarchy dominated by grabs for power and colonies by the Europeans, to the point where colonialism now is completely unthinkable, and where everyone in the world responds to the type of international disaster we've just seen in Bangladesh. I realize that much of what I say sounds very idealistic and perhaps unrealistic, but I think we have to be guided by our idealisms, even if we are not quite sure how they will work out. We must try to make them work.

QUESTION: President Bush's definition of a New World Order has been largely defined by crises: the Persian Gulf War, the plight of the Kurds, and the case of Bangladesh. It seems to me that there is a big distinction between that sort of New World Order and your approach, which is defined by a change in the day-to-day attitudes that go into making even domestic order. Could you elaborate on the distinction between these two visions?

AMBASSADOR McGHEE: I think we must discuss this problem because President Bush has not yet thought through and enunciated what he means by *New World Order*. As far as I know, his concept has been almost entirely related to the Persian Gulf War, a situation in which with no justification an independent state was occupied by a dictatorial regime, and something had to be done about it.

This is a rare circumstance. It may not happen again, certainly not to cause a war on this scale. I'm not sure we need to be worried too much about this particular eventuality. I would be more concerned about what we do about helping African countries who are sinking in poverty, losing their living standards, and facing high birth and death rates in an absolutely impossible situation.

We used to help Africa on quite a scale when we thought they were important to us in the Cold War. I hate to say it, but I think most of it was because of the Cold War. Now that the Cold War is gone, we have very little interest in helping these countries.

We give $15 billion worth of aid to countries of the world, 40 percent of which goes to Israel and Egypt because of the Arab-Israeli conflict. We give little to the sub-Saharan African countries. We are 16th, I think, among the nations in the amount of money we give for foreign assistance to others in terms of our GNP. I'm not sure that we are pulling our weight in the world today.

QUESTION: Don't you think that the best approach to this problem of world community is through human experience, just as we did in developing the common law—that is, to go by experience rather than by one preconceived grand plan?

AMBASSADOR McGHEE: I agree. I've used that analogy in various things I have written. The common law, as we know, is based on precedents set by individual cases, which together can then be used in other and more general applications. We could build up a basis in common international law of the types of situations in which a given country or a given person is accused of being in violation of the rights of the world community. There are certain things that the international community could tolerate, leaving to local or national jurisdiction. There are other crimes, however, that the community would and should not tolerate. They need not be only between nations; the scope of such law could be applied internally in nations, in the case of genocide, preparation for war, or in the denial of human rights.

I think you might reach a time when there is an international tribunal of the international community. If a complaint is brought, the case would be investigated by the equivalent of a grand jury, an indictment made and a trial conducted by the tribunal or the Security Council. One might help Cuba get rid of its dictatorship or Croatia become free from control by Yugoslavia on the basis that the case at hand is a violation of the rights of the international community. If the charge is sustained, the Security Council would call on the international community to take the necessary action.

QUESTION: How does the United Nations as it is presently constructed fit in with your idea of a world community?

AMBASSADOR McGHEE: I should have mentioned this, because the United Nations is obviously the best starting place to bring about international community. It has only recently shown itself quite effective in taking decisions, putting together, under United States leadership, the 125 nations that joined the coalition against Iraq. This was an extraordinary performance. It got the Iraqis out of Kuwait. There are many things the United Nations is now doing well which it should continue to do, such as taking care of refugees. My impression is that this has been done very well.

On the other hand, there are other situations that I believe could best be approached by some less bureaucratic approach, perhaps by some ad hoc regional organization, or by naming an international commission in a variety of circumstances the United Nations has not yet ventured into. Solutions to many problems might best be initiated by direct bilateral or multilateral approaches which might later be taken over by the United Nations in whole or in part in its operational phases.

QUESTION: Do you think the effects of the embargo against Iraq are a violation of human rights? I have heard children are dying because of the lack of food and sanitation.

AMBASSADOR McGHEE: That is an interesting question, and gives rise to the question of whether we thought through all the consequences of this war. No one predicted that the Kurdish revolt would occur. Even if we hoped it would, no one really knew if it would or what its consequences would be.

I believe that the people of Iraq, who were themselves victims of the war, were entitled to have their rights considered when decisions were made affecting imports of food and medicines.